SUPERFOODS FOR KIDS

SUPERFOODS FOR KIDS

Rena Patten

NEW
HOLLAND

To my very special tasting panel, my gorgeous
grandchildren, Madison, Kobe, Isaac, Hudson
and Cooper. This book is for you.
Love you more than you can imagine.
Yaya xxxxx

Contents

Introduction

Superfoods—you may be wondering what exactly this means.

The term, superfood, refers to a food source that is packed with lots of powerful antioxidants, vitamins, minerals, essential fatty acids and other nutrients.

Superfoods are considered to be beneficial to one's health by providing nutrients that naturally nourish the body without any side effects and without having to resort to taking supplements to get our daily quota of vitamins and minerals.

It is the unusually high amounts of nutrients that deems a food to be labeled as a superfood. Such foods are believed to help to reduce the risk of heart disease, cancer, high blood pressure, high cholesterol and obesity. They are said to rid the body of toxins and generally instil a feeling of physical and emotional wellbeing. There are lots of foods that fall under the umbrella of superfoods; not restricted to only ancient grains and seeds, dark leafy greens or other foods that are the 'buzz-foods' at the moment.

Simply put however, a superfood is any food that is naturally grown and fresh—food that has not been processed, filled with chemicals, additives, preservatives, artificial flavors, colors or enhancers.

The recipes in this book use superfoods that are appealing to children, whether they are meals for breakfast, school lunch boxes, every day lunches and dinners or special treats. And there's a chapter for new mums on preparing meals for babies when they first start on solids.

When I was thinking about recipes for this book I was guided by what my five grandchildren like to eat. Their ages range from under one to five.

We all want our children to grow up healthy, strong and happy so why not help them get an early start by teaching them the importance of eating food that is good for them (and appealing) from the very beginning.

By feeding children foods that are the best that nature can provide, they get the best start in life and develop good eating habits that will take them through to their adult lives.

As a bonus, eating fresh quality food will go a long way to providing their bodies with nutrients that will not only help to keep them healthy and may also help their bodies ward off diseases.

Without getting too technical and quoting facts and figures to convince anyone that eating good, healthy fresh food is a smart choice, children (and adults) need fresh food as nature intended without preservatives, artificial flavors or colors and processed to the point where the foods are almost unrecognizable.

Consuming the foods that are good for us on a regular basis is the key to a healthy and balanced diet. Eat well to keep healthy and avoid the processed, 'pre-prepared', pre-packaged food that we are surrounded by these days.

Food after all is fuel for our bodies. Good, clean, fresh and natural foods help bodies to grow strong, to rebuild cells, help our immune system and give us a better chance to lead a healthy life and help equip our bodies with the best chance possible to fight infections and disease.

With today's busy lifestyle, our lives become so hectic that it is much easier to pick up a meal that is already prepared, that will fill hungry tummies and provide instant comfort. These are times that we have all experienced. While the occasional takeaway meal is OK, this book includes easy-to-make, fast nutritious meals that are much healthier for your family.

Parents and carers have such a big influence on growing children. When it comes to food, they help mold the way children accept and treat food. It is during their younger years that they can learn to enjoy the foods that are good for them.

One of the greatest gifts that a parent can give their children from an early age is a love and appreciation of all food, where it comes from, how it is prepared and a love and feel of the warm environment in the family kitchen.

Children absolutely love to "help" in the kitchen; they love to be part of the cooking and and serving of food. This also makes for very special times spent together as a family.

Don't worry about the mess (let's be honest a lot of us do worry about this) and always remember that while there is no mess that cannot be cleaned up, the special bonding time lost can never be replaced. Children absolutely love this time and feel so proud of themselves when they see the finish product and listen to all the "oohs" and "ahhs" and the praise given to them about the delicious food they helped prepare.

My three children started helping out in the kitchen and cooking when they were very young. I remember I used to put an electric frying pan (do they even make these now?) on the kitchen counter and we would cook together. Then I would watch them eat straight from the pan. They were so chuffed that they had actually cooked the dish, they couldn't wait to try it.

It was such a special time for me and I hope for them. We used to talk about all the ingredients used and where they came from and, yes, usually quite a bit of mess came with it.

My daughters decided for themselves at a young age that they were going to be vegetarian and they still are today. My son, on the other hand, loved his meat and still does. These are choices that I think they were able to make because of their understanding of food.

My two older grandchildren who are now five have been encouraged to take an interest in helping in the kitchen. They are always so happy whenever they help make something.

My granddaughter, Madison, decided one day when she had just turned four that she was going to make a salad for her grandfather. So, with a plastic knife in hand she proceeded to cut all the salad ingredients (there were some very odd shapes I must say!) and made this enormous salad.

As she was leaving to go home, she asked me to take a video of gramps eating the salad and to send it to her. She wanted to see his reaction. She was so tickled pink by gramps' reaction

that she wanted to make a salad every time she came over. This went on for months.

My grandson, Kobe, at the age of three, decided that he liked to go "shopping" in my kitchen and would invariably go home every time he came over with a shopping bag that he had filled with whatever fresh fruit and vegetables took his fancy. He would then very proudly let me know what everything was used for.

I can't wait for my other three grand-babies, Isaac, Hudson and Cooper, to start doing their own thing in my kitchen when they get a little older although I must say they already know where the fruit bowl is.

These are irreplaceable moments for me and, at the same time, I know the kids are learning what food is, what is good for them to eat, what they can have at any time or as a special treat every now and then, and what they are just not allowed to have because their parents have said so.

When cooking the recipes from this book, you will find that they are all easy to prepare and use readily available ingredients.

In the baby food chapter, I have included food that can be quickly prepared and frozen. There are recipes in the main section that would be suitable for babies as well.

There are recipes that are gluten/wheat free for children who have allergies; these have been marked accordingly. Remember to check additives in certain foods such as prepared, off the shelf sauces used in recipes to see if they contain gluten and/or wheat.

I hope you will be able to experience many joys cooking with your children and grandchildren as they grow.

Rena Patten

BREAKFAST

Chia and Orange Pudding with Cherries
Sweet Potato and Spinach Pancakes
Apple, Cucumber and Kale Smoothie
Banana, Honey and Chocolate Smoothie
Banana and Chia Muffins
Cherry, Blueberry, Orange and Chia Smoothie
Corn Fritters
Spinach and Cheese Omelet Wraps
Breakfast Cereal Mix

Chia and Orange Pudding with Cherries

(Gluten/Wheat Free)

Serves 2-3

250 ml (8 fl oz) milk
4 tablespoons chia seeds
1 tablespoon honey or maple
   syrup
3 tablespoons fresh orange
   juice, strained
1 teaspoon vanilla bean
   paste or vanilla extract
1 teaspoon orange zest

TOPPING
30 g (1 oz) flaked almonds
2 tablespoons puffed quinoa
250 g (4 oz) frozen cherries
5 tablespoon water
1–2 teaspoon raw sugar
2 teaspoon lemon juice

1. Place the milk, chia seeds, honey, orange juice, zest and vanilla into a bowl or a glass jar with a tight fitting lid and mix together. Make sure you stir the bottom of the bowl to ensure the honey dissolves and all the ingredients have combined. If using a jar, put the lid on tightly and shake vigorously.
2. Leave to stand for about 5 minutes then stir vigorously again and repeat this process one more time.
3. Place in the refrigerator and leave to set overnight.
4. Serve topped with some cherry syrup and a good sprinkle of toasted almonds and puffed quinoa.
5. To prepare the topping, lightly toast the flaked almonds and puffed quinoa in a small non-stick frying pan. Shake and toss the pan regularly so that the nuts and quinoa don't burn. Remove from the heat, transfer to a small bowl and set aside.
6. Place cherries into a small saucepan with the water, sugar and lemon juice. Bring to the boil, reduce the heat and simmer on a low heat until the cherries soften and the liquid is a syrupy consistency.

This is lovely for breakfast and can be served either in individual bowls or in small jars with a tight fitting lid. If prepared in jars, the pudding becomes portable and is great to take to school. If taking to school, I would use plastic jars.

Sweet Potato and Spinach Pancakes

Makes about 12 pancakes

2 tablespoons extra virgin
   olive oil
1 small red (Spanish) onion,
   finely chopped
1 clove garlic, finely grated
2 good handfuls baby
   spinach, chopped
125 g (4 oz) self-rising (self-
   raising) flour
½ teaspoon ground cumin
1 teaspoon baking powder
500 g (16 oz) sweet potato
   (kumera), cooked and
   mashed
2 extra large eggs
375 ml (12 fl oz) milk
salt and freshly cracked black
   pepper
butter or extra virgin olive oil
maple syrup

1. Heat the oil in a large frying pan and sauté the onion until soft. Stir in the garlic and spinach and cook for 3–5 minutes until the spinach has wilted. Remove from the heat, place into a bowl and cool slightly.
2. Sift the flour, cumin and baking powder together and add to the spinach with the potato.
3. Whisk together the eggs and milk and season with salt and pepper if you wish.
4. Pour into the flour and vegetable mixture and stir well until all the ingredients are thoroughly mixed together and you have a thick batter.
5. Heat a non-stick frying pan on medium heat until hot and brush with butter or oil.
6. Pour about 3–4 tablespoons of the batter at a time into the pan and cook the pancake until bubbles start to appear and the top is set, about 2–3 minutes.
7. Flip over and cook until the other side is set. Keep the pancakes warm as you repeat until all the batter is used.
8. Serve with maple syrup drizzled over.

I like to cook the sweet potato by baking it whole with the skin on in the oven until soft when tested with a skewer. Peel when cool enough to handle then mash with a fork. You can also boil or steam the potato if you prefer.
If preparing these for breakfast on a school day, you can do most of the preparation the night before up to the stage where you add the milk and egg mixture.

Apple, Cucumber and Kale Smoothie

(Gluten/Wheat Free)

Makes 1 L (32 fl oz)

1 large stalk of kale
1 large Lebanese cucumber,
    sliced
1 banana, peeled and sliced
375 ml (12 fl oz) unsweetened
    apple juice
1 small red apple, cored and
    chopped
2 teaspoons honey
1 tablespoon lemon juice
ice cubes

1. Thoroughly wash the kale. Remove and discard the stalk and roughly chop the leaves.
2. Place kale into a blender with all the other ingredients and blend until smooth, thick and creamy.
3. Taste and adjust the level of sweetness used to suit your taste. Serve immediately.

This is a very refreshing tasting smoothie that children will love.

Banana, Honey and Chocolate Smoothie

(Gluten/Wheat Free)

Makes about 625 ml (21 fl oz)

500 ml (16 fl oz) unsweetened
   almond milk
1 large ripe banana
2 tablespoons honey
1 tablespoon organic raw
   cacao powder
2 teaspoons quinoa flakes
   should be 2 teaspoons
2 teaspoons extra virgin
   coconut oil
1 teaspoon vanilla bean
   paste
ice cubes

1. Place all of the ingredients into a blender and blend until thick, smooth and creamy.
2. Vary the sweetness to suit your taste and serve immediately.

Kids love this chocolate drink and it is packed with goodness including the raw cacao which is very high in antioxidants.

Banana and Chia Muffins

Makes 12

3 large ripe bananas
1 tablespoon lemon juice
½ teaspoon baking soda
   (bicarbonate soda)
125 g (4 oz) butter, room
   temperature
90 g (3 oz) organic coconut
   sugar
2 extra large eggs
40 g (1½ oz) almond meal
200 g (7oz) self-rising flour
½ teaspoon baking powder
2 tablespoon black chia
   seeds
125 ml (4 fl oz) milk
1 teaspoon vanilla bean
   paste or extract

LEMON ICING (OPTIONAL)
75 g (2½ oz) icing sugar,
   sifted
1–2 tablespoons lemon juice

1. Preheat the oven to 180°C (350°F) and place and line a 12-cup muffin pan with paper muffin cases.
2. Peel and finely mash the bananas with a fork then stir in the lemon juice and baking soda and set aside. The bananas will become light and fluffy at this stage.
3. Blend the butter and sugar together with electric beaters until light and creamy.
4. Beat in the eggs, one at a time, and then fold in the almond meal.
5. Sift the flour with the baking powder and fold into the mixture with the chia seeds, bananas, milk and vanilla.
6. Pour the mixture into the muffin cases and bake for about 25 minutes or until a skewer comes out clean when inserted. Remove muffins from the tin and cool on a wire rack.
7. To make the icing, mix all the ingredients together starting with the only a little lemon juice adding more until you have a smooth pouring consistency.
8. Serve warm (or cold) without icing or drizzle with a little of the lemon icing.

I find the amount of sugar above to be enough however you may need to adjust the level of sweetness and add a little more.

Cherry, Blueberry, Orange and Chia Smoothie

(Gluten/Wheat Free)

150 g (5 oz) frozen cherries
150 g (5 oz) frozen
  blueberries
juice of 2 oranges
1 cup coconut water
1 tablespoon maple syrup
1 tablespoon chia seeds

1. Place all ingredients into a blender and blend until thick, smooth and creamy.
2. Vary the amount of sweetener to suit your taste and add some ice cubes or extra coconut water if you would like a thinner consistency.

Corn Fritters

Serves 4

45 g (1½ oz) red quinoa, rinsed and drained

165 ml (5½ fl oz) water

6 stalks Cavolo Nero (Tuscan) kale, washed and stalk removed

4 scallions (spring onions), finely chopped

150 g (5 oz) self-rising flour

½ teaspoon baking powder

125 ml (4 fl oz) buttermilk

2 extra large eggs

1 x 400 g (14 oz) can creamed corn

200 g (7 oz) cooked corn kernels

salt and pepper

olive oil

1. Place quinoa into a small saucepan with the water. Bring to the boil. Reduce heat to very low, cover and simmer for about 12–15 minutes until cooked and all the water has been absorbed. Remove from the heat and cool.
2. Place the kale leaves into a bowl with boiling water from a recently boiled kettle. Leave in the water for about 2–3 minutes. Drain, squeeze dry then finely chop.
3. Combine the cooled quinoa and the kale with all the other ingredients except for the oil and mix well.
4. Heat a little oil in a non-stick frying pan on medium heat until hot.
5. Place about 2 tablespoons of the mixture into the hot oil and cook for about 2 minutes until bubbles start forming on the top.
6. Gently flip and cook for another minute on the other side or so until the fritters are firm to the touch and cooked through.
7. Remove from the heat and keep warm. Cook the remaining batter the same way.
8. Serve with your favorite dipping sauce like maple syrup.

For a gluten/wheat free alternative, these fritters can be prepared using quinoa flour. You can add some chopped ham or bacon to the batter if you like. These fritters make great vegetarian sliders (mini burgers). You may wish to cook double the amount of quinoa and freeze half the cooked quantity for use another time.

Spinach and Cheese Omelet Wraps

Serves 2–4

1–2 teaspoons extra virgin olive oil

3 scallions (shallots)

60 g (2 oz) baby spinach leaves

salt

1 teaspoon butter

4 extra large eggs

1 tablespoon homemade tomato dipping sauce (p. 67)

45 g (1½ oz) grated tasty cheese

2 wraps

1. Heat the oil in a medium sized non-stick frying pan and sauté scallions until soft and just starting to change color.
2. Add the spinach, season with a little salt and cook until the spinach wilts. Stir in the butter.
3. Whisk the eggs with the homemade tomato dipping sauce and pour over the spinach. Make sure the spinach is evenly dispersed within the eggs.
4. Sprinkle the cheese on top and cook the omelet until set gently moving the eggs around whilst cooking to make sure they set quickly and don't dry out.
5. When the omelet is cooked, remove from the pan and divide into two portions.
6. In the meantime, heat another non-stick frying pan or flat sandwich press until hot.
7. Place each portion of omelet along the centre of each wrap and fold over to enclose.
8. Place onto the heated frying pan or sandwich press and cook for about a minute on each side to seal and lightly toast.
9. Cut in half and serve.

Baby kale can be substituted for the spinach. A little hint: if using a sandwich press, line the inside with a folded piece of non-stick paper and place the wrap in the middle of the paper. This protects your sandwich press and lessens the cleaning up afterwards.

Breakfast Cereal Mix

(Gluten/Wheat Free)

150g (5 oz) red quinoa, rinsed and drained

375 ml (12 fl oz) water

125 g (4 oz) quinoa flakes

125 g (4 oz) whole blanched almonds

75 g (2½ oz) peppitas (pumpkin) seeds

75 g (2½ oz) sunflower seeds

60 g (2 oz) sesame seeds

2 teaspoons ground cinnamon

½ teaspoon ground nutmeg

1 tablespoon vanilla paste or extract

100 ml (2¾ fl oz) maple syrup

60 g (2 oz) light brown sugar, tightly packed

90 ml (3 fl oz) honey

2 tablespoons vegetable or extra light olive oil

150 g (5 oz) golden raisins

125 g (4 oz) dried cranberries

1. Place quinoa into a small saucepan with the water. Bring to the boil, reduce the heat and simmer for 10 minutes until all the water is absorbed. Remove from the heat, uncover and cool completely.
2. Preheat oven to 160°C (325°F) and line 2 large baking trays with non-stick baking paper.
3. In a large bowl mix together the quinoa flakes, cooled quinoa, almonds, pepitas, sunflower and sesame seeds, cinnamon and nutmeg.
4. Add the vanilla, maple syrup, brown sugar, honey and oil and mix really well as you want all the ingredients to be completely coated.
5. Spread the mixture out evenly over the 2 trays in a single layer and bake for about 30–40 minutes until crisp and crunchy and a rich golden color. Stir once or twice through the baking time making sure you keep the mix evenly distributed in the tray.
6. Remove from the oven and cool, then stir in the raisins and cranberries and when completely cold, store in an airtight container.
7. Serve with milk, or yogurt (or both) or sprinkle over porridge.

This is one of those mixes that is good to have on hand. It is not only great for breakfast, you can grab a handful of this at anytime. Good in school or work lunches. If you don't have maple syrup, golden syrup will work. Keep an eye on the mix whilst in the oven as it can burn easily. I have used the red quinoa in this recipe purely for the added crunch that you get from the darker grain.

SCHOOL LUNCHES

Turkey and Quinoa "Lollipops"
Cornbread
Spinach, Kale and Cheese Wraps
Sausage, Spinach and Cheese Muffins
Courgette and Carrot Slice
Rice Paper Rolls
Savory Kale and Feta Muffins
Ham, Broccoli and Cheese Muffins
Sushi Balls
Date, Cacao and Orange Energy Balls
Cranberry and Almond Bites
Apricot, Cashew and Coconut Power Balls

Turkey and Quinoa "Lollipops"

(Gluten/Wheat Free)

Makes about 20–25

90 g (3 oz) quinoa, rinsed and
   drained
250 g (8 fl oz) water
3 stalks kale
500 g (16 oz) turkey mince
4 scallions (spring onions),
   very finely sliced
2 cloves garlic, finely grated
1½ teaspoons dried thyme
2 tablespoons homemade
   tomato dipping sauce
   (p. 67)
salt and freshly ground black
   pepper
25 wooden lollipop sticks

1. Place quinoa in a small saucepan with the water. Bring to the boil, then reduce heat, cover and simmer for 10 minutes until all the water is absorbed. Remove from the heat and cool.
2. In the meantime, thoroughly wash the kale. Remove and discard the stalk. Chop the leaves very finely and set aside.
3. Place mince in a bowl with the scallions, garlic, thyme and homemade tomato dipping sauce. Season with salt and pepper to taste.
4. Add the cooled quinoa and kale and mix really well to combine all of the ingredients.
5. Take about 2 tablespoons of the turkey mixture and shape into a thick round patty. Carefully and gently insert a wooden stick into the patty so as to form a "lollipop".
6. Heat a little olive oil in a large non-stick frying pan until medium-hot, place the "lollipops" into the pan without overcrowding. Flatten a little and cook the until browned all over and the meat is cooked. These can also be grilled/broiled.
7. Serve with homemade tomato dipping sauce or any favorite sauce.

These turkey "sausages" can be eaten hot or cold and are not only ideal for school lunches but are great as finger food for parties and picnics. If you do not want to cook the quantity shown above at one time, the mixture can be prepared and frozen in small batches.

Cornbread

Serves 6–8

150 g (5 oz) self-rising flour
180 g (6 oz) fine cornmeal
  (polenta)
½ teaspoon bicarbonate
  soda
½ teaspoon baking powder
4 scallions (spring onions),
  finely sliced
150 g (5 oz) frozen corn,
  thawed
125 g (4 oz) frozen peas,
  thawed
salt
freshly cracked pepper
  (optional)
300 ml (10 fl oz) buttermilk
2 extra large eggs
1 tablespoon maple syrup
75 ml (2½ oz) light olive oil

1. Preheat the oven to 180°C (350°F) and brush a 23 cm (9 inch) square non-stick cake tin with a little oil then line the bottom with non-stick baking paper.
2. Sift flour, baking soda and baking powder into a large bowl. Add the cornmeal and mix well.
3. Stir in the scallions, corn and peas. Season with salt and pepper.
4. Whisk buttermilk, eggs and oil together and pour into the dry ingredients. Mix well.
5. Pour into the prepared cake tin and bake for 25–35 minutes until golden and a skewer comes out clean when tested.
6. Cool in the tin for about 10 minutes before removing on to a wire rack to cool.
7. Slice into desired sizes and shapes and serve.

For a little fun (something that kids seem to love), I sometimes cut the cornbread using novelty cookie cutters of all shapes and sizes or bake in small novelty-shaped tins.

Spinach, Kale and Cheese Wraps

Serves 4

2 tablespoons extra virgin olive oil

4 scallions (spring onions), thinly sliced

1 clove garlic, grated

500 g (16 oz) frozen spinach, thawed

250 g (8 oz) frozen kale, thawed

90 g (3 oz) feta cheese, crumbled

90 g (3 oz) ricotta cheese

1 tablespoon grated Parmesan cheese

4 wraps (wholemeal or white)

1. Heat the oil in a medium frying pan and sauté the scallions until soft. Stir in the garlic and cook for a few seconds.
2. Squeeze as much moisture from the spinach and kale as possible and add to the pan.
3. Cook for about 5 minutes stirring and combining the spinach and kale together well. Cool slightly then stir in the feta, ricotta and Parmesan and mix well. Check for seasoning at this stage and adjust by adding a little salt if necessary.
4. Divide mixture into 4 portions and spread each portion along half a wrap. Fold over the other half and press down to seal.
5. Heat a large non-stick pan until hot. (A flat sandwich press works well if you have one.) Cook the folded wrap in the pan or sandwich press until lightly browned on both sides.
6. Cut in half or into 3 triangles and serve.

These are almost like a Turkish pida/gozleme but much easier and quicker to prepare. They are great to take with you anywhere and kids love them.

If you can't find frozen kale use about 4 large fresh stalks of kale instead. If using fresh kale, thoroughly wash the kale, remove and discard the stalk and finely chop the leaves.

Sausage, Spinach and Cheese Muffins

(Gluten/Wheat Free)

Makes 12

125 g (4 oz) quinoa flour
1 teaspoon gluten-free
   baking powder
1 teaspoon baking soda
   (bicarbonate of soda)
1–2 teaspoon light olive oil
250 g (8 oz) sausages, skin
   removed
1 medium courgette
   (zucchini), coarsely grated
1 onion, coarsely grated
1 clove garlic, grated
75 g (2½ oz) grated tasty,
   matured cheese
5 eggs, lightly beaten
60 ml (2 fl oz) extra-light olive
   oil
30 g (1 oz) baby spinach
salt and freshly ground
   pepper

1. Preheat oven to 180°C (350°F) and line a 12-cup muffin tin with paper cases.
2. Sift the flour, baking powder and baking soda together and set aside.
3. Heat the oil in a non-stick frying pan and lightly brown the sausage meat breaking up any lumps until you have a fine mince consistency. Drain and discard any excess oil.
4. Place the mince into a bowl with the courgette, onion, garlic and cheese.
5. Finely chop the spinach and add to the bowl. Mix in the eggs and oil.
6. Fold in the flour mixture and season with salt and pepper. Make sure all the ingredients are mixed together well.
7. Pour the mixture into the prepared muffins tins and bake for about 20–25 minutes until golden and cooked when tested with a skewer.

These are delicious eaten warm or cold and are also good for a breakfast on the run. Use whatever sausage is a favorite. Italian-flavored sausages work really well in this recipe.

Courgette and Carrot Slice

Serves 6

500 g (16 oz) courgette (zucchini), coarsely grated

150 g (5 oz) carrot, coarsely grated

1 onion, grated

2 cloves garlic, grated

4 scallions (spring onions), finely sliced

6 eggs

75 ml (2½ fl oz) grape seed oil

125 g (4 oz) grated tasty/matured cheese

150 g (5 oz) self-rising flour

1 teaspoon baking powder

salt and freshly cracked pepper

2–3 extra medium courgette (zucchini)

1. Preheat oven to 180°C (350°F) and lightly grease 25cm (10 inch) square non-stick cake tine or baking dish. Line the bottom with non-stick baking paper.
2. Combine the courgette with the carrot, onion, garlic, scallions, eggs and oil.
3. Mix in the cheese and season with salt and pepper to taste.
4. Sift the flour with the baking powder then fold into the courgette and carrots and gently mix together until all the ingredients are combined.
5. Pour into the baking dish and flatten to even out the top.
6. Top and tail the extra courgette, slice thinly diagonally and arrange the slices on top of the mixture.
7. Place in the oven and bake for about 30–35 minutes until golden brown and set. Test with a skewer to make sure it is cooked right through.
8. Allow to rest for at least 10 minutes before serving if it is to be eaten warm. When using for school lunches, cool completely before cutting into squares or bars.

This slice can be eaten warm or cold which is why it is ideal for school lunches and picnics.

Rice Paper Rolls

(Gluten/Wheat Free)

Makes 8

200 g (7 oz) quinoa, rinsed
  and drained
500 ml (16 fl oz) water
1 avocado, peeled
1 Lebanese cucumber,
  coarsely grated
1 carrot, coarsely grated
1 tablespoon chia seeds
1 tablespoon fresh basil,
  chopped
1 tablespoon fresh mint,
  chopped
150 g (5 oz) cooked chicken,
  finely shredded (optional)
1–2 teaspoons rice vinegar
salt and freshly cracked
  pepper
8 rice paper wrappers
tamari soy sauce

1. Place quinoa into a small saucepan with the water. Bring to the boil. Reduce the heat, cover and simmer for 10 minutes until all the water is absorbed. Remove from the heat and cool. (You will not need all this amount of quinoa when cooked. Freeze the remaining quinoa for later use—it freezes beautifully.)

2. Squeeze as much moisture out of the cucumber as you can. Roughly mash the avocado and place into a bowl with the cucumber, carrot, chia seeds, herbs and chicken (if used) into a bowl and gently mix together.

3. Stir in about a third to half of the cooled quinoa and as much rice vinegar as you like. Season with salt and pepper. Divide mixture into 8 portions.

4. Fill a large shallow bowl with warm water and dip each wrapper, one at a time, into the water to soften, about 20 seconds (or as per packet instructions).

5. Place the softened wrapper flat onto a damp tea towel on the kitchen benchtop. Place a portion of the quinoa mixture in a straight line across the center of the wrapper leaving about a 5 cm (2 inch) edge uncovered.

6. Fold the uncovered sides over the filling and gently roll into a tight roll to enclose the filling. Repeat this process with all the paper rolls.

7. Serve the rolls with some soy sauce or your favorite dipping sauce.

When packing these for school lunches include a freezer block in the lunch box to keep rice rolls cool especially if using the chicken in the filling.

Savory Kale and Feta Muffins

Makes 12

6 stalks Cavolo Nero (Tuscan) kale

150 g (5 oz) fire roasted peppers (capsicums), store bought

90 g (3 oz) feta cheese

2 scallions (spring onions), finely sliced

1 clove garlic, grated

2–3 tablespoons Parmesan cheese, grated

300 g (10 oz) self-rising flour

2 extra large eggs, lightly beaten

250 ml (8 fl oz) milk

125 g (4 oz) butter, melted

1. Preheat the oven to 200°C (400°F) and grease a 12-cup non-stick muffin tin.
2. Thoroughly wash the kale then remove and discard the entire stalk. Wrap the leaves in a clean tea towel to dry then chop very finely.
3. Drain and finely chop the peppers then add to a bowl with the kale. Crumble in the feta cheese.
4. Stir in the scallions, garlic and as much Parmesan cheese as you like. Add the flour and lightly mix to combine.
5. Stir in the eggs, milk and butter and gently mix together until all the ingredients are combined.
6. Spoon the mixture into the prepared muffin tin and bake for about 15 minutes or until the skewer comes out clean when tested.
7. Leave muffins to cool slightly in tins for about 5 minutes before lifting out onto a wire rack to cool.

If you make as mini muffins, this recipe will make about 30. My grandchildren love the mini muffins and take them to preschool for lunch. They freeze well so they are easy to go from freezer to school lunch boxes.

Ham, Broccoli and Cheese Muffins

Makes 12–14

150 g (5 oz) self-rising flour

350 g (11½ oz) courgettes (zucchini), coarsely grated

1 onion, coarsely grated

90 g (3 oz) broccoli florets, stalk removed, finely chopped

90 g (3 oz) cheddar or tasty cheese, grated

180 g (6 oz) low-fat cottage cheese

2 tablespoon grated parmesan cheese

5 eggs, lightly beaten

60 ml (2 fl oz) extra light olive oil

salt and freshly ground pepper

90 g (3 oz) ham, chopped into small pieces

6–7 cherry tomatoes, halved

1. Preheat oven to 200°C (400F°)and grease a 12- or 14-cup muffin tin.
2. Sift the flour into a large bowl. Add the courgette, broccoli, onion, cheddar cheese, cottage cheese and Parmesan. Stir to combine.
3. Stir in the eggs and oil and season with salt and pepper. Give the mixture a good stir then fold in the ham.
4. Pour the mixture into the prepared muffin tin and top each muffin with a tomato half.
5. Bake for about 20–30 minutes until golden and cooked when tested with a skewer.

For a vegetarian option, leave out the ham or if catering for both vegetarians and non-vegetarians, fold the ham in half of the mixture before baking.

Sushi Balls

(Gluten/Wheat Free)

Makes about 30

250 g (8 oz) sushi rice
375 ml (12 fl oz) water
1 tablespoon sugar
2 tablespoons rice wine
  vinegar
30 g (1 oz) seasoned
  seaweed flakes
salt to taste

1. Rinse rice under cold running water, drain and place into a saucepan with the water.
2. Bring to the boil, reduce heat, cover and simmer for about 12–15 minutes until all the water is absorbed.
3. In the meantime, dissolve sugar in the vinegar and set aside.
4. Remove the rice from the heat. Stir in the seaweed flakes (you can add as much or as little as you like). Taste and season with a little salt if you think necessary and leave to stand covered for about 5 minutes.
5. Place the rice into a non-metallic bowl and stir in the vinegar mixture then gently mix to combine all the ingredients together. Cool the rice until cool enough to handle.
6. Take spoonfuls of the rice and, using wet hands, roll into balls to whatever size you like. You can make big ones or smaller ones—I find the size of a walnut to be a good manageable size.
7. Store in a covered container in the refrigerator until ready to serve.

Kids absolutely love these. They are especially good for school lunches. Add a small freezer block to the lunch box especially in warmer months. These are also great to serve at children's parties.

Date, Cacao, and Orange Energy Balls

(Gluten/Wheat Free)

Makes 20–24

150 g (5 oz) Medjool dates, pitted

125 g (4 oz) almonds, with skin on

3 tablespoons organic raw cacao powder

zest of 1 large orange

3–4 tablespoons orange juice

2 tablespoons organic raw coconut oil, melted

2 tablespoons maple syrup

60 g (2 oz) moist coconut flakes or shredded coconut

1–2 tablespoon chia seeds

1. Soak the dates in hot water for 5 minutes to soften then drain well and reserve the water.
2. In the meantime, place the almonds in a food processor and process until finely chopped.
3. Add the dates, cacao powder, zest, orange juice, coconut oil, maple syrup and coconut flakes to the food processor and process until the mixture comes together and you have a paste-like consistency. If mixture is too thick and not processing smoothly, add a little of the drained water from the dates to loosen.
4. Transfer mixture into a bowl. Stir in the chia seeds and mix until well combined. Taste to check for sweetness and add a little more maple syrup if desired.
5. Wet the palms of your hands with cold water and roll the mixture into walnut-sized balls or whatever size you prefer.
6. Refrigerate for at least 3–4 hours before serving.
7. Store these in the refrigerator in an airtight container.

Medjool dates are the best you can get and readily available. They are very moist with no added sugar and have no additives: perfect for these energy balls.

Cranberry and Almond Bites

(Gluten/Wheat Free)

Makes about 24

125 g (4 oz) raw almonds with skin on

125 g (4 oz) dried cranberries

90 g (3 oz) golden raisins

1 teaspoon fresh orange zest

2–3 tablespoons organic raw coconut oil, melted

15 g (½ oz) puffed quinoa or puffed amaranth

1. Place almonds into a food processor and process until finely chopped. Add the cranberries, raisins, orange zest and coconut oil and continue processing until the nuts and fruit are all finely chopped and you have a slightly sticky mixture with a little texture to it.

2. Transfer this mixture into a bowl and add the quinoa or amaranth puffs. Mix all the ingredients together—your hands are probably best for this. Press the mixture together as you mix so that it holds firmly together.

3. Roll the mixture into bite size rounds or a size that best suits you and refrigerate until set.

4. Store in a covered container in the refrigerator for up to 3–4 weeks.

Amaranth is an ancient grain that has been around for centuries. Puffed amaranth is used just as you would puffed quinoa and is available at most health food stores.

Apricot, Cashew and Coconut Power Balls

(Gluten/Wheat Free)

Makes 24

150 g (5oz) Medjool dates, pitted

150 g (5 oz) raw cashews

125 g (4oz) dried apricots, roughly chopped

60 g (2 oz) dried cranberries

3 tablespoons organic raw coconut oil

3 tablespoons pure raw cacao powder

1 teaspoon vanilla bean paste

shredded coconut

1. Place the dates in a bowl. Pour over boiling water and soak for 5 minutes to soften. Drain well and reserve the liquid to use later (3–4 tablespoons).
2. Place cashews into a food processor and process until they are finely chopped.
3. Add dates, apricots, cranberries, coconut oil, cacao, vanilla and some of the date soaking liquid and process until all the fruit and nuts are finely chopped.
4. Add more soaking liquid as needed and continue processing until you have a fine and moist paste, but not too wet.
5. Lightly wet your hands and roll the mixture into balls the size of a small walnut or whatever size you prefer. Roll the balls in the shredded coconut.
6. Refrigerate until they become firm then store in a covered container.

Check for sweetness before you roll these as there has been no sweetener added to this mixture. If you do not find them sweet enough, add some maple syrup or honey. Medjool dates are the best you can buy, do not have added sugar or additives and are available from most supermarkets.

LUNCHES AND DINNERS

Fried Chicken
Potato Wedges
Chicken Kebabs with Kale and Bacon
Chicken Tacos with Kale-Slaw and Avocado Salsa
Crumbed Fish Fingers
Baked Chicken Nuggets
Super Sliders with Homemade Tomato Dipping Sauce
Vegetable and Beef Filo Snails
Halloween Peppers with Mexican Pasta
San Choy Bow
Creamy Chicken and Leek Soup
Sweet Potato, Pumpkin and Quinoa Soup
Flourless Crusted Pizza
Spaghetti Bolognaise
Crumbed Lamb Cutlets
Ham, Corn and Pea Soup with Noodles
Crunchy Tuna and Spinach Mornay
Chicken and Vegetable Loaf
Chicken Fried Quinoa
Baked Potatoes with Mexican Beef
Pumpkin and Courgette Rissoto
Chicken Stir-Fry
Veggie Burgers
Baked Risotto with Corn, Bacon and Kale
Tempura Vegetables

Fried Chicken

(Gluten/Wheat Free)

Serves 4

4 large chicken Maryland (leg and thigh), skin removed
300 ml (10 fl oz) buttermilk
125 g (4 oz) quinoa flakes
1 teaspoon sweet paprika
1 teaspoon dried thyme leaves
1 teaspoon ground turmeric
½ teaspoon ground cumin
pinch of salt
drizzle olive oil
lemon juice for serving

1. Buy even sized chicken pieces. Make 2 incisions along each cutlet part of the chicken pieces and 1 on the drumsticks. You can leave the Maryland whole or separate the drumstick from the cutlet.
2. Place into a bowl with the buttermilk and mix well to completely cover the chicken making sure you rub it well into each incision.
3. Leave to marinate in the refrigerator for a few hours; at least 6–8 hours or overnight.
4. Preheat oven to 200°C (400°F) and line a baking tray with non-stick baking paper.
5. Prepare the coating by mixing together the quinoa flakes with the sweet paprika, thyme, turmeric, cumin and a little salt. Make sure all the spices are evenly distributed through the quinoa flakes.
6. Give the chicken a little shake to remove any excess buttermilk and transfer to kitchen paper towels and very lightly pat dry.
7. Coat the chicken completely with the coating mixture pressing it into the chicken. Place on the baking tray.
8. Lightly drizzle each piece of chicken with a very small amount of oil and bake in the oven for 45–55 minutes or until the chicken is cooked, golden brown and crunchy.
9. Leave to rest for 5–10 minutes before serving with a squeeze of lemon juice. Delicious!

Invite the kids' friends over for this fried chicken meal and feel no guilt whatsoever knowing that it is not only home-made and baked but also gluten/wheat free.

Potato Wedges

(Gluten/Wheat Free)

Serves 4

1 kg (2 lb) potatoes
2 tablespoons chia seeds
1 tablespoon ground cumin
1 teaspoon ground paprika
½ teaspoon curry powder
  (optional)
½ teaspoon ground turmeric
1 teaspoon garlic salt
½ teaspoon dry thyme leaves
2 tablespoons organic raw
  coconut oil (or extra virgin
  olive oil)
light sour cream
sweet chili sauce (optional)
homemade tomato dipping
  sauce (optional) p. 67.

1. Wash and scrub the potatoes then cut into wedges lengthways leaving the skin on.
2. Drop into a pot of boiling water, bring back to the boil and cook for 10 minutes.
3. In the meantime, preheat the oven to 200°C (400°F) and line a large baking tray with non-stick baking paper.
4. Mix together the chia seeds, cumin, paprika, curry (if used), turmeric, garlic salt, thyme leaves and set aside.
5. When potatoes are ready, drain well. Place on paper towels and lightly pat dry—the potatoes should be as dry as possible before coating with the other ingredients.
6. Pour the coconut oil over the potatoes and coat completely.
7. Sprinkle the spice mixture over the potatoes so that the potatoes are completely coated.
8. Spread the potatoes onto the prepared tray in a single layer and bake in the oven for 30–40 minutes until golden, crisp and tender.
9. Serve with sour cream and a sweet chili sauce and/or homemade tomato dipping sauce (if used).

Extra virgin olive oil can be substituted for the coconut oil.

Chicken Kebabs with Kale and Bacon

Serves 6–8

8–10 Cavolo Nero kale stalks
12 large chicken tenderloins
dried thyme leaves
6 slices streaky bacon (or
  sliced ham), cut in half
  lengthways
extra virgin olive oil
½ lemon, juiced
salt and pepper

1. To start, soak 6 to 8 bamboo skewers in cold water for 2 hours to stop the skewers from burning during cooking.
2. In the meantime, thoroughly wash the kale, remove the thick stalks and place the leaves into a bowl. Cover the kale with hot water from a recently-boiled kettle and leave to stand for about 3–5 minutes.
3. Drain well and lightly toss through a little extra virgin olive oil and balsamic vinegar. Set aside. Depending on the size of the leaves, you will need enough to cover the 12 tenderloins.
4. On a chopping board, gently pound the chicken fillets on the underside with the flat side of a mallet until thin.
5. Season the tenderloin. Sprinkle with a little thyme and cover each one with kale and top with a slice of bacon. Roll each one as tightly as possible and cut in half.
6. Secure the rolls on bamboo skewers, 3–4 half rolls per skewer should be plenty. Drizzle each kebab with a little olive oil and season with salt and pepper if you wish.
7. Heat a large frying pan or griddle pan until hot and cook the kebabs for about 10 minutes until golden. Keep turning the kebabs over on all sides during cooking to make sure that the chicken is cooked through.
8. Remove from heat, loosely cover with foil and allow to rest for about 5 minutes before serving. Test one of the kebab rolls by cutting in half to make sure they are cooked properly (while resting the chicken will continue to cook).
9. Serve with your favorite sauce.

Chicken Tacos with Kale-Slaw and Avocado Salsa

(Gluten/Wheat Free)

Serves 3–6

500 g/ (16 oz) chicken tenderloins
½ teaspoon ground cumin
½ teaspoon ground oregano
½ teaspoon ground sweet paprika
1 clove garlic, finely chopped
pinch of chili (optional)
1 teaspoon extra olive oil
pinch of salt
6–8 corn taco shells

AVOCADO SALSA
1 large avocado, seed removed and
   chopped into small pieces
1 tomato, finely chopped
½ small red onion, finely chopped
extra virgin olive oil
lime juice, to taste
salt and black pepper

KALE-SLAW
6–8 stalks Cavolo Nero (Tuscan) kale
1 tablespoon red wine vinegar
1 medium carrot, coarsely grated
½ red onion, halved and finely sliced
1 stalk celery, finely sliced
3 scallions (shallots), finely sliced
salt and freshly cracked pepper
2 tablespoons gluten-free mayonnaise
1–2 teaspoons extra virgin olive oil

1. Trim the chicken tenderloins and place in a bowl with the cumin, oregano, paprika, garlic, chili (if used) and oil. Season with a little salt to taste. Leave to marinate for about 1 hour if possible.
2. Heat a large non-stick frying pan or griddle pan and cook the tenderloins for 3–4 minutes each side depending on size, then shred. You can also broil (grill) if you prefer.
3. To make the avocado salsa, simply combine all the ingredients together.
4. To make the kale-slaw, thoroughly wash the kale, remove and discard most of the lower thick part of the stalk and finely shred the leaves.
5. Place the kale into a bowl and pour in the red wine vinegar. Using your hands rub the vinegar into the kale. This helps to soften the kale.
6. Add the carrots, onion, celery, scallions and mayonnaise. Season with salt and pepper and mix well to combine.
7. Assemble the tacos by placing some kale-slaw on the bottom of each taco shell followed by a strip or two of chicken then top with the avocado salsa and a dollop of sour cream if you wish.

Crumbed Fish Fingers

Serves 4

125 g (4 oz) panko breadcrumbs

1 large clove garlic, finely grated

zest of 1 lemon

1 tablespoon fresh chives, chopped

1 tablespoon fresh flat leaf parsley, chopped

1 tablespoon white chia seeds

salt and freshly cracked black pepper

500 g (16 oz) white boneless fish fillets

1 extra large egg, lightly beaten

extra light olive oil for shallow frying

lemon or lime juice

tartare sauce (optional)

1. Combine the breadcrumbs with the garlic, lemon zest, chives, parsley, chia seeds, salt and pepper.
2. Mix well making sure the garlic and lemon zest are rubbed through the breadcrumbs so that they are evenly dispersed.
3. Cut the fish fillets into fingers without too much wastage then dip into the beaten egg. Coat the fish with the crumb mixture pressing firmly to coat the fish completely.
4. Heat the oil in a large frying pan on medium heat until hot and gently shallow fry the fillets until cooked and golden, approximately 3–5 minutes each side depending on the thickness of the fish.
5. Remove from the pan on to kitchen paper then serve hot with lemon juice and tartare sauce if using.

Panko are Japanese-style breadcrumbs, coarsely ground into airy, large flakes that give fried foods a light, crunchy coating. The flakes tend to stay crispier longer when cooked than standard breadcrumbs because they don't absorb as much grease. For a gluten/wheat free alternative, substitute the panko breadcrumbs for quinoa flakes or a mixture of quinoa and amaranth flakes. Choose whichever fish fillets you prefer. John Dory, Ling or Snapper are three that work well in this recipe.

Baked Chicken Nuggets

Gluten/Wheat Free)

Serves 4–6

500 g (16 oz) chicken
  tenderloins
125 g (4 oz) quinoa flakes
2 teaspoons ground sweet
  paprika
1½ tablespoons sesame
  seeds
salt to taste (optional)
1–2 eggs, lightly beaten
oil spray
homemade tomato dipping
  sauce (optional), p. 67
lemon juice (optional)

1. Preheat the oven to 190°C (375°F) and line a large baking tray with non-stick baking paper.
2. Trim the chicken tenderloins and cube each strip into large bite size pieces.
3. Mix together the flakes, paprika, sesame seeds and salt (if used).
4. Dip all the chicken pieces into the beaten egg then coat them well with the flake mixture pressing the coating firmly on to the chicken.
5. Place onto the prepared baking tray in a single layer and lightly spray the nuggets with the oil.
6. Bake for about 10 minutes on each side until golden and crisp.
7. Serve with a salad and your preferred dipping sauce and/or a squeeze of lemon juice.

Super Sliders with Homemade Tomato Dipping Sauce

Makes 12

2 large stalks kale
500 g (16 oz) minced beef
1 small onion, grated
1 clove garlic, finely grated
1 large courgette (zucchini),
  coarsely grated
1 tablespoon chia seeds
2 tablespoons quinoa flakes
1 tablespoon tomato paste
½ teaspoon dried oregano
salt and pepper
12 small slider (burger) buns
lettuce leaves
tomato slices
avocado slices

HOMEMADE TOMATO DIPPING SAUCE

25 g (8 oz) organic tomato
  paste concentrate
60 ml (3 fl oz) pure maple syrup
40 ml (1½ fl oz) white wine
  vinegar
90 ml (3 fl oz) water
2 teaspoons onion powder
1 teaspoon sea salt
½ teaspoon garlic powder
½ teaspoon mustard powder
¼ teaspoon ground cloves

1. To make tomato dipping sauce, place all the ingredients into a blender or food processor and process until all the ingredients are combined and smooth. Place into a glass jar with a lid and refrigerate for at least 4 hours before using, overnight even better to allow all the flavors to develop.
2. To make the sliders, thoroughly wash the kale. Remove and discard the tough stalk then chop the leaves very finely.
3. Place into a bowl with the mince, onion, garlic, courgette, chia seeds, quinoa flakes, tomato paste, oregano, salt and pepper.
4. Mix to thoroughly combine then shape into small flat patties or whatever size you prefer.
5. Heat a large non-stick frying pan and coat with a little extra virgin olive oil. Cook the patties on both sides. If you flatten them out (rather than rounded), the patties will cook more evenly throughout. Alternatively you can grill, barbecue or cook the patties on a griddle pan.
6. To assemble the sliders, lightly toast the buns, layer with some lettuce leaves, slices of tomato and avocado, top with the patties and serve with tomato dipping sauce or any other favorite sauce.

Keep the dipping sauce in the refrigerator at all times. Use as an alternative to store-bought ketchup (tomato sauce).

Vegetable and Beef Filo Snails

Makes 8

500 g (16 oz) butternut
  pumpkin (squash)

1 onion, finely chopped

425 g (15 oz) beef mince

2 cloves garlic, finely
  chopped

125 g (4 oz) frozen peas,
  thawed

1 x 400 g (14 oz) can creamed
  corn

60 g (2 oz) fresh baby spinach
  leaves

1 teaspoon dried thyme
  leaves

salt and pepper

16 sheets filo pastry

sesame seeds

1. Peel pumpkin and cut into very small pieces and set aside.
2. Heat oil in a large frying pan and cook onion until soft and golden. Add the mince and cook until the meat is sealed all over.
3. Add the pumpkin and continue cooking on medium heat until the pumpkin is soft.
4. Stir in the garlic, peas, corn and thyme. Season with salt and pepper and continue cooking until the peas are cooked.
5. Add the spinach leaves and cook until they wilt then remove from the heat and cool.
6. Preheat oven to 200° (400°F) and line a large baking tray with non-stick baking paper.
7. Lie flat 1 sheet of filo and lightly brush with olive oil then top with another sheet of filo so that you have 2 sheets together for each snail to work with.
8. Divide the vegetable mixture into 6 portions then place 1 portion along the longer edge of the pastry.
9. Fold over part of the sides to enclose the filling then gently roll over the filo until you have one long cylinder. Brush the edge at the end with some oil and then lightly brush the whole cylinder with a little oil.
10. Very gently twirl the filo roll into a round coil and place onto the prepared tray. Repeat with the other 5 portions.
11. Sprinkle 'the snails' with sesame seeds and bake for about 20–30 minutes until golden. Serve with a salad.

For a vegetarian alternative, replace the mince with some crumbled feta or goat's cheese.

Halloween Peppers with Mexican Pasta

Serves 6

6 stalks kale

6 peppers (capsicum), stalk intact

2 tablespoon olive oil

1 leek or onion, finely copped

3 cloves garlic, chopped

2 teaspoons ground oregano

1 tablespoon ground cumin

2 teaspoons ground paprika

2 tablespoons tomato paste

180 g (6 oz) frozen corn

250 g (8oz) butternut pumpkin (squash), diced into small pieces

1 x 400 g (14 oz) can diced tomatoes

150 g (5 oz) small pasta (elbow or shell)

salt to taste

750 ml (24 fl oz) boiling water

1 x 400 g (14 oz) can red kidney beans, drained and rinsed

grated tasty matured cheese

1. Thoroughly wash the kale. Remove and discard the tough stalk and finely chop the leaves. Set aside.
2. Preheat oven to 200°C (400°F) and line a baking tray with non-stick baking paper.
3. Cut a lid from the peppers and remove the seeds and membranes from inside. Using a small sharp knife cut out a Halloween face in each of the peppers.
4. Place the lid back on the peppers. Brush or spray with a little olive oil and roast in the oven for about 15–20 minutes until the peppers are tender but still holding their shape. Remove from the oven and allow to cool. There may be some. Discard any liquid built up inside the peppers while they cooked before filling.
5. Meanwhile, heat the oil in a large deep frying pan and sauté the leek until soft and slightly golden.
6. Stir in the garlic and cook until fragrant then add the oregano, cumin, paprika and cook for about 30 seconds.
7. Stir in tomato paste and cook for 1 minute. Add the kale, corn, pumpkin, undrained tomatoes, pasta, salt and water. Bring to the boil, reduce heat, cover and simmer on low heat for about 10–15 minutes until pasta is cooked. Add more water if necessary during cooking.
8. Stir in the red kidney beans and cook on low heat until the beans are heated through.
9. Fill the peppers with the pasta filling. Sprinkle with some cheese, cover with their lid and return to the oven for just long enough to melt the cheese.

Choose fresh, firm, well-shaped peppers (capsicums) that are a fairly good size, stand upright and have the stalk intact. If a bit wobbly, cut a thin slice from the bottom to level them off

San Choy Bow

(Gluten /Wheat Free)

Serves 6

4 stalks kale

2 tablespoons peanut/olive oil

500 g (16 oz) chicken or pork
mince

4 scallions (shallots), finely
sliced

2 cloves garlic, finely grated

1 tablespoon fresh ginger,
grated

90 g (3 oz) fresh beans, finely
sliced

½ red pepper (capsicum), finely
chopped

1 small carrot, finely diced

1 teaspoon palm or coconut
sugar

2–3 tablespoons fish sauce

2 tablespoons gluten-free soy
sauce

1 teaspoon sesame oil

3 tablespoons water

2–3 tablespoons fresh cilantro
(coriander), optional

150 g (5 oz) bean sprouts

juice of 1 lime (optional)

6 lettuce leaves

1. Thoroughly wash the kale. Remove and discard the
   lower thick part of the stalk. Chop the leaves finely and
   set aside.
2. Heat oil in a wok or a large frying pan. Add mince and
   sauté until it is sealed all over breaking up any lumps as
   it cooks.
3. Stir in scallions, garlic and ginger and cook for about 1
   minute until fragrant, stirring constantly.
4. Add the beans, peppers, carrot and kale and stir well.
   Stir in the fish and soy sauce, sesame oil and water cook
   for about 5–7 minutes until the vegetables are tender
   and the chicken is cooked.
5. Chop cilantro and stir through with bean sprouts and as
   much lime juice as you like.
6. Trim lettuce leaves with scissors to form cups. Choose
   crisp tender leaves.
7. Serve the mince in the lettuce cups.

Cos/romaine lettuce works really well in this recipe.

Creamy Chicken and Leek Soup

Serves 6

1 tablespoon butter

1–2 tablespoons extra virgin olive oil

2 large leeks, washed and sliced

3 celery stalks, roughly chopped

1 brown onion, chopped

6 chicken thigh cutlets about 1.25 kg (2 lb 13 oz)

2 L (4 pt) chicken stock or water

pinch of ground cloves

10–12 peppercorns

180 ml (6 fl oz) red quinoa, rinsed and drained

Salt and pepper

125 ml (4 fl oz) cream

1. In a large saucepan, melt the butter and heat the oil until hot, then sauté the leeks, celery and onion until they soften and collapse and just start to take on some color.
2. Remove the skin from the chicken (optional) and add to the pot with the stock, cloves and peppercorns.
3. Bring to the boil, reduce the heat and simmer for about 30–40 minutes until chicken is cooked. Skim and remove any froth that rises during cooking.
4. Remove the chicken from the pot and set aside. Puree the soup and bring back to the boil.
5. When the soup is boiling, add the quinoa and season with salt. Reduce the heat, cover and simmer for about 20–30 minutes until the quinoa is cooked.
6. In the meantime, if you have left the skin on during cooking, remove the skin from the chicken and shred the meat into pieces.
7. Add the shredded chicken and cream to the soup and stir well. Taste and adjust the seasoning if necessary then continue to simmer on very, very low heat for 5 minutes until the chicken and cream have heated through.
8. Serve with a good grind of freshly cracked black pepper.

Thigh cutlets are the thigh with the back rib part of the bone removed and only the larger thigh bone left in. Because there is only one bone, I find using stock instead of water will give a far richer and tastier soup. I do like to use chicken thigh cutlets in this recipe as I feel thighs are better for soups and with just the larger bone in them the risk of finding smaller bones in the soup is less. But of course you can use whatever chicken pieces you prefer.

Sweet Potato, Pumpkin and Quinoa Soup

(Gluten/Wheat Free)

Serves 6

1 tablespoon olive oil

1 large onion, chopped

2–3 cloves garlic, chopped

1 teaspoon ground cumin

½ teaspoon ground
coriander

750 g (24 oz) sweet potato
(kumera)

750 g (24 oz) butternut
pumpkin (squash)

2 L (64 fl oz) hot chicken or
vegetable stock

salt and freshly cracked black
pepper

90 g (3oz) red quinoa, rinsed
and drained

light sour cream

lemon juice (optional)

1. Heat the oil in a large saucepan and sauté onion until soft. Add the garlic and cook for about 30 seconds then stir in the cumin and coriander and cook until fragrant.

2. Peel the sweet potato and pumpkin. Roughly cube and add to the saucepan with the stock and season to taste. Bring to the boil, reduce the heat, cover and simmer for 20–30 minutes until the vegetables are tender.

3. Puree soup and bring back to the boil. Add the quinoa, reduce the heat, cover and simmer for 20–25 minutes until the quinoa is cooked and soft. Leave to stand for at least 10–15 minutes before serving. This allows the quinoa to soften more and for the soup to thicken.

4. Serve with a dollop of sour cream and lemon juice if using.

When using the red or black quinoa in soups, the cooking time once the quinoa is added is usually longer than if using white quinoa. When cooked in a dense liquid quinoa in general requires longer cooking time than if cooked in water.

Flourless Crusted Pizza

(Gluten/Wheat Free)

Serves 2–4

4 stalks kale

750 g (26½ oz) cauliflower florets

2 tablespoons quinoa flakes

1 large clove garlic, finely grated

2 extra large eggs

3 tablespoons Parmesan cheese, grated

TOPPINGS

150 g (5 oz) tomato paste

1 clove garlic, finely grated

1 teaspoon dried oregano leaves

1 teaspoon extra virgin olive oil

5 mozzarella slices

black olives

grape tomatoes, halved (optional)

fresh basil leaves

1. Thoroughly wash the kale. Remove and discard the stem and roughly chop the leaves. Place the cauliflower and kale into a food processor and process until very finely chopped.

2. Place into a microwave-safe dish, cover with microwave-safe lid and cook until the cauliflower and kale are very tender, about 8–10 minutes on high. Choose a microwavable dish that has a large surface rather than a bowl.

3. Place into a fine sieve and squeeze out as much moisture as you can with your hands. Leave to cool—the cauliflower and kale need to be quite dry.

4. Preheat the oven to 200°C (400° F) and line a 30 cm (12 inch) pizza tray with non-stick baking paper.

5. Combine the cauliflower and kale with the quinoa flakes, garlic, egg and cheese and mix well. Spread the mixture on the lined tray. Spread a little thicker around the edge so as to make a crusty edge when cooked.

6. Bake for about 25–30 minutes until golden and crisp around the edges. Remove from the oven.

7. Mix together the tomato paste, garlic, oregano and oil and spread over the base of the pizza avoiding the edge. Top with slices of mozzarella cheese, olives and tomatoes (if used).

8. Return to the oven and bake for a further 5–8 minutes until the cheese has melted. Remove from the oven, garnish with basil leaves and rest for a few minutes before slicing.

This is not like your regular pizza base made from flour. It is quite soft, very light, tasty, has minimal amount of carbohydrates and of course, is gluten and wheat free. You can vary the toppings to suit your taste. If using a conventional oven, you may need to set the temperature a little higher and cook the base for a little longer.

Spaghetti Bolognaise

Serves 6

2 tablespoons extra virgin
olive oil

1 large onion, finely chopped

750 g (24 oz) lean minced
beef

4–6 large stalks Cavolo Nero
kale

3 cloves garlic, finely
chopped

3 tablespoons tomato paste

1 teaspoon dried oregano
leaves

1 large courgette (zucchini),
coarsely grated

1 large carrot peeled and
coarsely grated

750 ml (24 fl oz) tomato
passata sauce

625 ml (20 fl oz) hot water

pinch of salt (optional)

180 g (6 oz) spaghetti

Parmesan cheese, grated
(optional)

1. Heat the oil in a large saucepan and sauté onion on medium-high heat until golden.
2. Add the minced beef and continue cooking on medium-high heat until browned all over. Break up any lumps as you go.
3. In the meantime, thoroughly wash the kale. Remove the thick stalk, chop the leaves very finely and set aside.
4. Once the meat has browned, stir in the garlic and cook for about 1 minute until fragrant. Add the tomato paste and oregano and cook for 1–2 minutes.
5. Stir in the courgette, carrot and kale, mix well then pour in the passata and the water and season with a little salt if you wish.
6. Bring to the boil, reduce the heat. Simmer on low heat covered for about 45 minutes until the sauce has reduced and thickened.
7. In the meantime, bring a large saucepan of salted (optional) water to the boil. Add the spaghetti and stir occasionally to stop the strands from sticking together. Cook the pasta following packet directions or until al dente.
8. Divide spaghetti into bowls and spoon over bolognaise sauce and sprinkle with Parmesan if using.

This is a family favorite. I usually make double or triple the quantity and freeze it in small amounts ready for the unexpected visit of my little people who never seem to tire of eating spaghetti with this sauce. My daughters used to give this to their babies from about 10 months old. The sauce will keep in the refrigerator for about 4–5 days.

Crumbed Lamb Cutlets

(Gluten/Wheat Free)

Serves 4–6

12 lamb cutlets
100 g (3½ oz) quinoa flakes
2–3 cloves garlic, finely
  grated
zest of 1 lemon
2 teaspoons dried oregano
  leaves
salt
freshly cracked black pepper
  (optional)
45 g (1½ oz) quinoa flour
2 eggs, lightly beaten
olive oil for shallow frying

1. Trim cutlets of any excess fat and lightly pound with a mallet to flatten.
2. Combine the quinoa flakes with the garlic, lemon zest, oregano, salt and pepper. Set aside. Make sure the garlic is evenly dispersed through the flakes.
3. Lightly dust each cutlet with some flour. Dip in the beaten egg then press into the quinoa flake mixture and coat well.
4. Heat the oil in a large frying pan until hot. Gently shallow fry the cutlets on low-medium heat until golden, approximately 3–4 minutes each side.
5. Serve hot with a squeeze of lemon juice.

Kids love these and, as they are crumbed with quinoa flour and flakes, they are gluten/wheat free. Check the cooking time to ensure they are cooked to your likeness.

Ham, Corn and Pea Soup with Noodles

Serves 6

6 stalks kale

1–2 tablespoons extra virgin olive oil

150 g (5 oz) ham, cut into bite-sized pieces

2 medium leeks, washed and sliced

1 clove garlic, chopped

460 g (15½ oz) frozen corn

460 g (15½ oz) frozen peas

1.5 L (48 fl oz) hot chicken or vegetable stock

freshly cracked black pepper (optional)

90 g (3 oz) dried vermicelli pasta noodles

Parmesan cheese, freshly grated

1. Thoroughly wash the kale. Remove and discard the lower thicker part of stalk then chop the leaves and set aside.
2. In a large saucepan, heat the oil until hot then cook the ham until golden and crisp. Remove from the pot with a slotted spoon and set aside.
3. Add the leek and garlic to the saucepan and sauté until soft and just starting to take on some color. If necessary add a little more oil.
4. Stir in the kale, corn, peas and stock. Bring to the boil, reduce the heat, cover and simmer for about 15 minutes.
5. Break up the noodles into small pieces and add to the soup with the ham.
6. Bring back to the boil. Reduce the heat, cover and simmer for about 3–5 minutes until the noodles are cooked.
7. Turn off the heat and allow the soup to sit for about 10 minutes before serving with a good sprinkle of freshly-grated Parmesan cheese.

For a gluten/wheat free alternative, use rice vermicelli or quinoa instead of the vermicelli pasta noodles. If using quinoa, you will need to cook it for about 15–20 minutes and maybe add a little extra stock or water. Quinoa takes longer to cook when added to a soup.

Crunchy Tuna and Spinach Mornay

Serves 4–6

1 x 400 g (14 oz) tuna in brine or spring water

30 g (1 oz) butter

3 tablespoons all-purpose (plain) flour

½–1 teaspoon curry powder

425 ml (14 fl oz) low-fat milk

75 g (2½ oz) tasty cheese, grated

90 g (3 oz) baby spinach leaves

salt and pepper (optional)

TOPPING

60 g (2 oz) corn flakes

30 g (1 oz) popped quinoa or popped amaranth

90 g (3 oz) tasty cheese, grated (extra)

1. Preheat oven to 180°C (350°F).
2. Drain and flake the tuna and place in a medium casserole dish.
3. Melt butter in a saucepan then stir in the flour and curry powder to form a roux.
4. Slowly pour in the milk, stirring constantly until sauce starts to thicken and bubble.
5. Stir in the cheese and cook for about 2 minutes until cheese has melted into the sauce and the sauce is thick and bubbly.
6. Add the spinach and stir until the spinach wilts and blends into the sauce. Season with salt and pepper.
7. Pour the sauce over tuna and mix thoroughly to combine.
8. In a separate bowl, lightly crush the cornflakes and mix with the popped quinoa and extra cheese.
9. Sprinkle the corn flake mixture over the tuna, and bake for about 20 minutes until the top is golden and crunchy, the sauce is bubbly and the cheese has melted through the cornflake and quinoa topping.

You can substitute the flour with quinoa flour for a gluten/wheat free option. You can substitute the spinach leaves with kale. If using kale, wash thoroughly, remove the stalk and chop the leaves very finely.

Chicken and Vegetable Loaf

(Gluten/Wheat Free)

Serves 4–6

500 g (16 oz) chicken breast mince

125 g (4 oz) corn kernels

1 medium courgette (zucchini), coarsely grated

60 g (2 oz), red peppers (capsicum), finely chopped

3 tablespoons quinoa flakes

2 cloves garlic, finely grated

4 scallions (shallots), thinly sliced

1 tablespoon fresh parsley, finely chopped

1 teaspoon dried oregano leaves

1 teaspoon fresh thyme, finely chopped

2 eggs

salt and freshly ground pepper

quinoa flakes, extra

1. Preheat oven to 180°C (350°F). Lightly oil a 31 x 11 x 7.5 cm (12 x 4½ x 3 inch) loaf tin and line the bottom with non-stick baking paper. Make sure the paper comes right up the longer sides of the tin for easy removal of the loaf once cooked.
2. Lightly oil the baking paper and sprinkle with the extra quinoa flakes.
3. Mix the chicken mince with the corn, courgette, peppers, quinoa flakes, garlic, scallions, parsley, thyme, oregano and eggs. Season with salt and pepper.
4. Make sure mixture is thoroughly combined. Place into the loaf tin, sprinkle with extra quinoa flakes and bake for about 40–45 minutes or until golden on top and the chicken is cooked.
5. Allow to cool in the tin for 5–10 minutes before lifting out and serving.

This chicken loaf can be also eaten cold and makes a delicious sandwich filling. You can use chicken thigh or breast mince or even substitute with pork or turkey mince if you prefer.

Chicken Fried Quinoa

(Gluten/Wheat Free)

Serves 4–6

180 g (6 oz) quinoa, rinsed
and drained
500 ml (16 fl oz) water
1 tablespoon oil
2 eggs
1 teaspoon tamari soy sauce
1 tablespoon water
2 tablespoon oil, extra
½–1 teaspoon sesame oil
600 g (21 oz) chicken breast
fillets, thinly sliced
3 rashers bacon, rind
removed and diced
8 scallions (shallots), sliced
125 g (4 oz) frozen peas
200 g (7 oz) fresh baby corn
spears or 1 x 400 g (14 oz)
can, drained
2–3 tablespoons tamari soy
sauce

1. Place quinoa in a small saucepan with the water. Bring to the boil, then reduce the heat, cover and simmer for 10 minutes or until all the water is absorbed. Remove from the heat and spread out on a tray to cool and dry out completely. You can always do this in advance or use leftover cooked quinoa.

2. Lightly whisk the eggs with the soy sauce and water. Heat the oil in a wok until hot. Add the beaten eggs and swirl around to form an omelet.

3. When the eggs have set, tilt wok away from you and using a spatula, carefully roll up the omelet. Remove from the wok and slice into thin strips. Set aside.

4. Heat extra oil and sesame oil in the wok. Add the chicken and toss for about 3–4 minutes.

5. Add the bacon and continue cooking on high heat stirring constantly until the chicken is completely cooked and the bacon is crispy.

6. Add the scallions with as much of the green parts as possible. Add peas and corn spears and continue stirring for 2–4 minutes until peas have thawed.

7. Stir in the soy sauce and the quinoa and continue cooking for 3–4 minutes until quinoa is heated through. Stir in the egg strips and serve with an extra drizzle of soy sauce and chopped scallions.

This is a twist to the well-known and much-loved Asian fried rice—made with quinoa instead of rice. It is so much lighter to digest than the usual fried rice. You can use prawns instead of the chicken and bacon.

Baked Potatoes with Mexican Beef

(Gluten/Wheat Free)

Serves 4–6

6 medium–large brushed
  potatoes
2 tablespoons extra virgin olive
  oil
1 small onion, finely chopped
450 g (16 oz) minced beef
2 cloves garlic, finely chopped
1½ teaspoons ground cumin
1 teaspoon sweet paprika
1 teaspoon dried oregano
1–2 tablespoons tomato paste/
  puree
1 x 400 g (14 oz) can diced
  tomatoes, undrained
125 ml (4 fl oz) water
1 x 400 g (14 oz) can red kidney
  beans, undrained
75 g (2½ oz) baby spinach
  leaves, chopped
4–6 dollops light sour cream
3–4 tablespoons avocado,
  roughly mashed
freshly chopped cilantro
  (coriander), optional
1 lime, cut into thin wedges

1. Preheat the oven to 200°C (400°F). Wash and scrub the potatoes and bake with the skin on until soft and tender. Choose good-sized potatoes that are not small and preferably ones that are flat.
2. In the meantime, heat oil in a large deep frying pan and cook the onion until soft and golden.
3. Add the mince and continue cooking until browned. Stir in the garlic and cook for about 30 seconds.
4. Stir in the cumin, paprika, oregano and cook for a few seconds until fragrant then stir in the tomato paste/puree and cook for 1–2 minutes.
5. Add the diced tomatoes and water and simmer on low heat covered for 10 minutes.
6. Add the beans and spinach, season with salt and pepper if you wish, cover and continue cooking on low heat for about 10 minutes.
7. Stir in the cilantro (if used) and allow to cool slightly.
8. When the potatoes are cooked and cool enough to handle, remove a portion of the skin from the top of each one and scoop out about two-thirds of the potato. Place into a bowl and very lightly mash with a fork.
9. Fold the potato through the mince and fill each potato with the mince mixture piling it up high. Serve with avocado, a dollop of sour cream, cilantro leaves and slices of lime on the side.

Consider adding a little chili to the mince as it is cooking—very nice for kids who like a bit of spice. Depending on the size of the potatoes, you may have some mixture leftover. If you do, it can be heated up with an egg or two cooked in the mixture then served on toast.

Butternut Pumpkin and Courgette Risotto

(Gluten/Wheat Free)

Serves 4–6

500 g (16 oz) butternut
   pumpkin (squash)
1 tablespoon olive oil
1 onion, finely chopped
3 cloves garlic, finely grated
400 g (14 oz) Arborio rice
salt and freshly cracked
   pepper
350 g (11½ oz) courgette
   (zucchini), coarsely grated
1½ L (48 fl oz) hot chicken or
   vegetable stock
1 tablespoon butter, extra
2–3 tablespoons Parmesan
   cheese, freshly grated

*My grandmother always
used to say risotto waits for
no one; one has to be
at the table waiting for it to
be ready.*

1. Preheat the oven to 200°C (400F°) and line a baking tray with non-stick paper.
2. Peel the pumpkin. Remove the seeds and cube. Place on the baking tray. Lightly coat with a little olive oil and season with salt and pepper.
3. Bake for about 20–25 minutes until the pumpkin is tender and a little charred. Remove from the oven and set aside.
4. Heat oil in a large saucepan. Add the onion and sauté until soft. Stir in the garlic and cook for about 30 seconds.
5. Add the rice, stir well to coat with the other ingredients and cook for about 1–2 minutes until the rice becomes opaque. Season with salt and pepper and stir in the courgette.
6. In another pot, have the stock simmering on very low heat. Pour a ladleful of the hot stock into the rice and stir until all that liquid is absorbed.
7. Whilst stirring the rice, continue adding stock a ladleful at a time over low-med heat. Allow the stock to be absorbed before adding the next.
8. Cook until the risotto is soft and creamy, about 25–30 minutes. Taste and if it is cooked the way you like it, stir in the extra butter and Parmesan cheese. Gently stir through the pumpkin.
9. Taste and adjust the seasoning keeping in mind that the Parmesan cheese and stock (if using store bought) can be salty. Risotto should be soft, creamy—similar to porridge consistency.
10. Serve immediately.

Chicken Stir-Fry

(Gluten/Wheat Free)

Serves 4–6

750 g (26½ oz) chicken breast fillets, trimmed and sliced thinly

2 cloves garlic, finely chopped

1½ tablespoons kecap manis

1–2 tablespoons oil

½–1 teaspoon sesame oil

500 g (16 oz) broccoli, cut into florets

1 large red pepper (capsicum), de-seeded and diced

1 medium carrot, sliced diagonally

60 g (2 oz) snow peas, string removed

2 tablespoons tamari soy sauce

125 ml (4 oz) water

4–5 scallions (shallots), thickly sliced diagonally

bean sprouts

1. Place the chicken into a bowl with the garlic and kecap manis. Mix well and leave to marinate while you prepare the vegetables.
2. Heat oil and sesame oil in a wok or large deep-sided frying pan until hot. Add the chicken in two batches and stir-fry over high heat for 3–4 minutes until golden. Remove from the pan and set aside.
3. Add a little more oil to the wok if necessary then add the broccoli, pepper, carrot, snow peas and stir-fry for about 2 minutes.
4. Pour in the soy sauce and water and stir-fry for another 2–3 minutes or until vegetables are tender but still crisp.
5. Return the chicken to the pan with the scallions and toss for 2–3 minutes until chicken heated through and completely cooked.
6. Toss through as many bean sprouts as you like and serve over cooked rice or quinoa garnished with extra bean sprouts.

Kecap Manis is an Indonesian sweet soy sauce typically sold in Asian supermarkets. It may contain wheat. If you are gluten/wheat intolerant, you can mix equal parts of tamari soy sauce and brown sugar as a substitute.

Veggie Burgers

(Gluten/Wheat Free)

Makes 8

60 g (2 oz) quinoa, rinsed and
drained
125 ml (4fl oz) water
2 stalks kale
150 g (5 oz) broccoli florets,
cooked and chopped
4 scallions (spring onions),
finely chopped
1 clove garlic, finely grated
125 g (4 oz) frozen corn,
thawed
1 x 400 g can chickpeas,
drained and mashed
½ small red pepper
(capsicum), very finely
chopped
200 g (7 oz) sweet potato
(kumera), cooked
2 eggs
salt and pepper
8 burger buns
mayonnaise (optional)
lettuce leaves
slices of tomatoes

1. Place quinoa into a small saucepan with the water. Bring to the boil, reduce the heat, cover and simmer for 10 minutes until all the water is absorbed. Remove from the heat and cool. (You may need to add a little more water during cooking as such a small amount of quinoa tends to absorb the water before it is cooked.)
2. Preheat the oven to 200°C (400°F) and line a baking tray with non-stick paper.
3. Thoroughly wash the kale, remove the stalk and finely chop the leaves.
4. Chop the broccoli florets into small pieces and place into a bowl with the quinoa, kale, scallions, garlic, corn, chickpeas, red pepper and sweet potato. Combine together then add the eggs. Lightly season with salt and a little pepper and mix well.
5. Divide mixture into 8 and shape into patties. Place onto the prepared tray and bake for about 20–25 minutes.
6. Slice burger buns in half and lightly toast the inside. Spread a little mayonnaise on each bun if you are using it, top with a vegie patty, lettuce leaves, slices of tomato and your favorite sauce.

The patties are gluten/wheat free without the burger buns.

Baked Risotto with Corn, Bacon and Kale

Serves 4

3 large stalks kale
1–2 tablespoons extra virgin
   olive oil
150 g (5 oz) bacon, diced
1 medium onion, finely
   chopped
3 scallions (shallots), sliced
2–3 large cloves garlic, finely
   chopped
250 ml (8 fl oz) passata
   (puree)
250 g (9 oz) Arborio rice
salt and freshly cracked black
   pepper
1 L (32 fl oz) hot chicken
   stock
250 g (9 oz) frozen corn
knob of butter
3 tablespoons Parmesan
   cheese, grated
shaved parmesan cheese
lemon juice (optional)

1. Preheat the oven to 200°C (400°F). Thoroughly wash the kale. Remove and discard the stalk and finely chop the leaves. Set aside.
2. Heat the oil in a large saucepan. Add the bacon and cook until crisp. Start with 1 tablespoon of oil as the bacon will render some fat when cooking. Remove the bacon from the pan with a slotted spoon and set aside.
3. Add onion and scallions to the pan and cook on medium heat-high until soft and golden. Stir in the garlic and cook for another 30 seconds or so until fragrant.
4. Stir in the passata and rice. Season with a little salt and pepper keeping in mind that the stock (if using store bought) may be salty.
5. Pour in the stock. Give it a good stir, cover and bake in the oven for 20 minutes.
6. Add the frozen corn and kale. Stir well and bake for a further 10 minutes.
7. Remove from the oven. Stir in the butter, bacon and Parmesan cheese and leave to stand for 5–10 minutes. Before serving, garnish with shavings of Parmesan cheese. Add a squeeze of lemon juice and stir through the risotto if you wish.

This is such an easy risotto to make as you don't have to stand over the stove for 30-odd minutes adding in the stock a little at a time. Just throw it in the oven and get on with whatever else needs doing. It is also just as delicious without the bacon.

Tempura Vegetables

Serves 4–6

200 g (7 oz) orange sweet
  potato (kumera), unpeeled,
  cut in thin rounds
150 g (5 oz) broccoli florets
60 g (2 oz) string beans
60 g (2 oz) sugar snap peas
2 large courgette (zucchini)
1 large carrot
light olive oil for frying
sea salt

TEMPURA BATTER
180 g (6 oz) all-purpose
  (plain) flour
¼ teaspoon baking powder
  (bicarbonate of soda)
2–3 tablespoons corn starch
  (cornflour)
1 extra large egg
300 ml (10 fl oz) icy cold soda
  water
extra flour for dusting

1. Prepare the vegetables to have them ready before you start cooking.
2. Remove the string from the beans and snow peas and leave whole.
3. Slice the courgette and carrot diagonally, 5 mm (¼ inch) thick.
4. Sift the flour, corn starch and bicarbonate of soda. Lightly whisk in the egg and icy cold soda water.
5. Place the bowl with the batter over a larger bowl filled with ice cubes. This will keep the batter icy cold throughout the whole cooking process.
6. Heat the oil in a deep frying pan until hot, but not smoking hot.
7. Lightly dust the vegetables with the extra flour then dip into the batter and coat well.
8. Gently drop the vegetables into the hot oil and cook a few minutes until golden all over. It's best not to overcrowd the pan while cooking. Sprinkle with a little sea salt if you like and serve immediately.

The quantities mentioned for the vegetables are only a guide to the ratio of batter. You can use whatever other vegetables you prefer. Carrots, mushrooms and eggplant (aubergines) also work really well in this recipe. If you have an allergy to egg whites, this recipe will work using just the yolk.

SPECIAL TREATS

Chocolate Snack Squares
Creamy Coconut and Mango Pudding
Sticky Date Pudding
Chocolate Mousse
Raw Brownie Bites
Carob Bars
Chocolate, Mandarin and Cranberry Muffins
Chocolate Chip and Raisin Cookies on a Stick
Pistachio Cookies
Blueberry and Almond Friands
Maple Syrup, Coconut and Quinoa Cookies
Hot Chocolate
Blueberry and Chia Sorbet Icy Poles
Yogurt, Strawberry, Chia and Almond Icy Poles

Chocolate Snack Squares

(Gluten/Wheat Free)

Makes about 20

60 g (2 oz) coconut flour

1 teaspoon gluten-free baking powder

60 g (2 oz) quinoa flakes

125 g (4 oz) coconut sugar

2 tablespoons organic raw cacao powder

60 g (2 oz) slivered almonds

90 g (3 oz) peppitas (pumpkin) seeds

90 g (3 oz) sunflower seeds

2 tablespoons chia seeds

1 teaspoon ground cinnamon

125 g (4 oz) butter, melted

1 teaspoon vanilla bean paste

2 extra large eggs, lightly beaten

1. Preheat oven to 180°C (350°F) and lightly grease a 30 x 20 cm (12 x 8 inch) slice tin and line with baking paper.
2. Sift flour and baking powder into a large bowl. Stir in the quinoa flakes and sugar. Mix well making sure you break up any lumps in the sugar.
3. Add the cacao, almonds, peppitas, sunflower seeds, chia seeds and cinnamon and mix well to combine everything together.
4. Pour the melted butter, vanilla and eggs over the seed mixture and mix well by pressing and mixing all the ingredients together until they are combined and not dry.
5. Using the back of a spoon, press the mixture firmly and evenly into the prepared tin and bake for about 15–20 minutes until set.
6. Remove from the oven and leave to cool in the tin for about 10–15 minutes. Cut into desired sized bars. Leave to cool in the tin a little longer then carefully remove the slice with the paper and place on a cooling rack to cool completely
7. When cooled, for ease of transportation, wrap each bar in plastic wrap and store in an airtight container.

These bars are great when a quick snack is needed. Carob powder can be substituted for the cacao powder

Creamy Coconut and Mango Pudding

Serves 12

140 g (5 oz) quinoa grain, rinsed and drained

2 x 400 g (14 oz) cans coconut milk, plus extra 120 ml (4 fl oz)

150 g (5 oz) sugar

2 fresh mangoes

40 g (1½ oz) toasted coconut flakes

1. Place the quinoa in a large saucepan with all the coconut milk and the sugar. Bring to the boil, then reduce the heat, cover and simmer on low heat for 20–25 minutes, until thick and creamy.

2. Meanwhile, peel the mangoes. Thinly slice half of one to use as decoration later; set aside. Cut remaining mangoes into small pieces.

3. When the quinoa is soft and cooked, stir through the mango pieces and pour into individual bowls or a large serving bowl. Sprinkle with the toasted coconut and decorate with the slices of mango. Refrigerate before serving.

To toast the coconut flakes, place into a small non-stick frying pan and toast over a low heat—there's no need to add any oil or butter. This pudding is a favorite with everyone—it's absolutely delicious.

Sticky Date Pudding

Serves 12

500 g (17½ oz) Medjool
   dates, pitted
590 ml (20 fl oz) water
1 teaspoon baking soda
   (bicarbonate of soda)
250 g (9 oz) unsalted butter
250 g (9 oz) superfine (castor)
   sugar
4 extra large eggs
2 teaspoons vanilla extract
1 teaspoon ground cinnamon
250 g (9 oz) quinoa flour
2 teaspoons baking powder
strawberries, for garnish

CARAMEL SAUCE
200 g (7 oz) unsalted butter
400 g (14 oz) brown sugar
240 ml (8 fl oz) pouring cream
1 teaspoon vanilla extract

1. Place dates and water into a large saucepan and bring
   slowly to the boil. Reduce the heat and simmer for 1
   minute. Remove from heat. Stir in the baking soda— the
   mixture will froth up so make sure you use a big enough
   saucepan so it doesn't spill over. Set aside to cool—the
   mixture will thicken as it cools.
2. Preheat oven to 160°C (325°F) and grease 12-cup capacity
   baking pan.
3. Using electric beaters, cream the butter and sugar together
   until light. Beat in the eggs, one at a time, with the vanilla
   and cinnamon.
4. Sift the flour and baking powder and slowly incorporate
   with the creamed butter mixture. Fold in the cooled dates
   and divide cake mixture evenly between the prepared tins.
   Place tins on a baking tray and bake for 35–40 minutes.
   When cool, run a thin knife along the side of the molds to
   loosen the puddings, then invert onto a serving plate.
5. To make the caramel sauce, place all ingredients into a
   small saucepan and simmer for a few minutes until the
   sauce starts to bubble and thicken.
6. Serve puddings with lots of caramel sauce and a strawberry
   on top of each. You can cut the strawberries to make a fan
   shape for special effect.

Medjool dates are perfect for sticky date pudding as they are very moist
with no additives—available at most supermarkets.

Chocolate Mousse

(Gluten/Wheat Free)

Serves 2–4

45 g (1½ oz) raw cacao powder

125 ml (4 oz) coconut water

1 large ripe avocado, peeled and seed removed

2 teaspoons vanilla extract or vanilla bean paste

3 tablespoons honey

1 tablespoon pure organic raw coconut oil, melted

crushed toasted almond flakes

fresh strawberries

1. Mix the cacao powder and the coconut water together in a blender then add the avocado, vanilla, honey and coconut oil.
2. Puree until you have a very fine, whipped mixture. Keep in mind that the cacao powder is quite bitter so taste and adjust the level of sweetness at this stage.
3. Pour into individual dessert glasses or small coffee cups and refrigerate for at least 4 hours.
4. To toast the almond flakes, place almonds into a small non-stick frying pan and lightly toast over a medium heat until golden or roast in the oven. Cool then place in a plastic bag and lightly crush with a rolling pin.
5. Serve with the toasted almonds and strawberries.

Although this is a healthy dessert, it is quite rich so you may want to stretch this quantity to serve 4 people and serve it in small coffee cups or shot glasses. For something a little different, you can flavor this chocolate mousse with orange zest or a little freshly grated ginger added to the blender in step 1.

Raw Brownie Bites

(Gluten/Wheat Free)

Makes 20–24

250 g (9 oz) Medjool dates, pitted

150 g (5oz) almond meal

125 g (4 oz) slivered almonds

40 g (1½ oz) raw cacao powder

2 teaspoons vanilla extract

60 ml (2 fl oz) coconut water

3 tablespoon organic coconut oil, melted

extra raw cacao powder, for dusting

1. Grease and line a 9 x16 cm (6 x 7 inch) baking tin with non-stick baking paper. Make sure the paper extends over the edge of 2 sides so that you can easily lift the brownies out of the tin.
2. Place all the ingredients into a food processor and process until you have a smooth, thick paste. You may have to move the mixture around in the processor with a spatula a few times to ensure an even texture.
3. Lightly wet your hands and press the mixture firmly into the prepared tin.
4. Refrigerate for at least 6–8 hours for the mixture to set—overnight is best.
5. Before serving, dust with extra raw cacao powder and cut into bite-sized pieces.

Carob powder can be substituted for the raw cacao. Medjool dates are very moist and the best to use. They are available at supermarkets and specialty grocery stores.

Carob Bars

(Gluten/Wheat Free)

Makes about 12

90 g (3 oz) pure roasted
   carob powder
80 ml (2 fl oz) warm water
125 g (4 oz) butter
2 tablespoons golden syrup
1 teaspoon vanilla extract
45 g (1½ oz) puffed quinoa
45 g (1½ oz) slivered almonds
60 g (2 oz) dried sultanas
½ teaspoon ground
   cinnamon

1. Grease and line the bottom of a 26 x 8 cm (10 x 3 inch) bar baking tin with non-stick baking paper. Make sure the paper extends over the edge of 2 sides so that you can easily lift the bars out of the tin once they are ready.
2. Mix the carob powder and the water in a bowl and set aside.
3. Melt the butter in a small saucepan. Stir in the golden syrup then mix into the carob and water mixture with the vanilla.
4. Stir in the puffed quinoa, almonds, sultanas and cinnamon and mix until all the ingredients are totally covered.
5. Press the mixture firmly into the prepared tin and refrigerate for at least 6 hours, preferably overnight, until set. Cut into bars or slices to serve.
6. Store carob slices in the refrigerator in a covered container.

Carob is a great alternative to chocolate. It is available from most health food stores. Make sure you use pure good quality carob powder. Raw cacao can be substituted for the carob powder and the golden syrup can be substituted with carob syrup. If using raw cacao, you may have to adjust the level of sweetness as raw cacao can be quite bitter.

Chocolate, Mandarin and Cranberry Muffins

(Gluten/Wheat Free)

Makes 12

125 g (4 oz) almond meal

125 g (4 oz) coconut sugar

60 g (2 oz) quinoa flour

2 tablespoons organic raw
  cacao powder

1 teaspoon baking powder

125 g (4 oz) dried cranberries

zest of 2 large mandarins
  (clementines)

125 ml (4 fl oz) mandarin
  (clementine) juice

125 g (4 oz) unsalted butter,
  melted and cooled

1 teaspoon vanilla bean
  paste

4 large eggwhites

MANDARIN ICING

3 tablespoons icing sugar,
  sifted

1 tablespoon mandarin
  (clementine) juice

1. Preheat the oven to 180°C (350°F). Line a 12-cup muffin tin with paper cases.
2. Place the almond meal, coconut sugar, flour, cacao and baking powder into a bowl. Whisk well breaking up any lumps in the mixture that may have formed.
3. Mix in the cranberries and zest then lightly stir in the mandarin juice, butter and vanilla.
4. Beat the eggwhites until foamy and soft peaks form. Gently fold into the mixture. Spoon the mixture evenly into the prepared patty tins.
5. Bake for approximately 20 minutes until cooked. When tested with a metal skewer, the skewer should be clean.
6. Remove from the oven and cool completely.
7. To make the icing, mix the icing sugar with as much mandarin juice as needed to make a slightly thick but runny consistency. Pour over the cooled muffins.
8. Store in a covered biscuit tin or a plastic container with a good fitting lid.

Chocolate Chip and Raisin Cookies on a Stick

Makes 12

250 g (8 oz) self-rising flour

½ teaspoon baking powder

3 tablespoons organic raw cacao powder

125 g (4 oz) white chocolate chips

60 g (2 oz) golden raisins

125 g (4 oz) butter, room temperature

75 g (2½ oz) coconut sugar

1 teaspoon vanilla extract

2 extra large eggs

3 tablespoons low-fat milk

12 wooden lollipop sticks

1. Preheat the oven to 180°C (350°F) and line 2 baking trays with non-stick baking paper.
2. Sift together the flour, baking powder and cacao then stir in the chocolate chips and raisins. Set aside.
3. Cream the butter and coconut sugar together until light and creamy.
4. Beat in the vanilla and eggs then fold in the flour mixture and the milk and mix until well combined. Mixture will be soft and sticky.
5. Divide mixture into 12 and with slightly wet hands, shape each into a round cookie and place onto the prepared tray.
6. Insert a wooden stick into the middle of each cookie (biscuit). Cookies should not be crowded in the trays; usually 6 per tray is more than enough.
7. Bake for about 11–12 minutes. Do not overcook; they should be a little soft when taken out of the oven.
8. Cool completely on the tray before removing them and storing in an airtight container.

Quinoa flour can be substituted for regular flour. If using quinoa flour, use 150 g (5 oz) flour plus 1 teaspoon baking powder and ½ teaspoon baking sode (bicarbonate soda). Wooden lollipop sticks can be purchased where craft materials are sold.

Pistachio Cookies

Makes 20–24

125 g (4 oz) quinoa flour

1½ teaspoons baking powder

1 teaspoon baking soda (bicarbonate soda)

90 g (3 oz) quinoa flakes

125 g (4 oz) shelled, unsalted pistachio nuts, chopped but not too finely

200 g (7 oz) superfine (castor) sugar

150 g (5 oz) unsalted butter, melted

1 teaspoon vanilla bean paste or extract

1 extra large egg, lightly beaten

1. Preheat the oven to 180°C (350°F) and line two baking trays with non-stick baking paper.
2. Sift the flour, baking powder and baking soda into a bowl then stir in the quinoa flakes, chopped pistachio nuts and sugar.
3. Pour in the melted butter and vanilla. Mix well, then stir in the egg and mix everything until you have a mixture that holds together when pressed with your fingertips.
4. Take spoonfuls of the mixture, the size of a walnut, and lightly roll into a ball then place onto prepared trays. Flatten slightly. The biscuits will spread during baking so leave enough space between each one on the tray.
5. Bake for 10–12 minutes until golden. Cool completely on the trays before removing and storing in an airtight container. They should be crisp on the outside and chewy in the middle.

These biscuits are very easy to make are extremely popular with little ones and grownups alike. I often make a double quantity as they disappear too fast. They are great for school lunches or picnics or to take when visiting friends or family.

Blueberry and Almond Friands

(Gluten/Wheat Free)

Makes 9

125 g (4 oz) almond meal

250 g (8 oz) pure icing sugar, sifted

45 g (1½ oz) quinoa flour

125 g (4 oz) unsalted butter, melted and cooled

½ teaspoon vanilla extract

4 large egg whites

1 punnet fresh blueberries

1. Preheat the oven to 180°C (325°F). Grease a 9-cup friand tin with butter.
2. Place the almond meal, icing sugar and quinoa flour into a bowl. Whisk to break up any lumps of mixture that may have formed.
3. Lightly mix in the butter and vanilla extract.
4. Beat the egg whites until foamy and soft peaks form. Gently fold into the mixture.
5. Spoon the mixture evenly into the prepared tin.
6. Place 6–8 blueberries around the center of each friand and lightly press them into the mixture.
7. Bake for approximately 25 minutes until lightly browned and cooked through when tested with a metal skewer.

You can substitute the blueberries with mixed berries, raspberries or blackberries.

Maple Syrup, Coconut and Quinoa Cookies

(Gluten/Wheat Free)

Makes 20–23

90 g (3 oz) quinoa flakes
3 tablespoons puffed quinoa
125 g (4 oz) quinoa flour
100 g (3½ oz) coconut sugar
1 teaspoon baking powder
1 teaspoon baking soda
   (bicarbonate soda)
75 g (2½ oz) shredded
   coconut
125 g (4 oz) butter, melted
2 tablespoons maple syrup
2 teaspoons vanilla extract
2 tablespoons hot water

1. Preheat the oven to 160°C (325°F) and grease and line 2 baking trays with non-stick baking paper.
2. Place quinoa flakes, puffed quinoa, flour, coconut sugar, baking powder and baking soda into a bowl. Mix well then stir in the coconut.
3. Melt the butter then stir in the maple syrup, vanilla and hot water. Mix well.
4. Pour the melted butter mixture into the dry ingredients and mix until thoroughly combined.
5. Place spoonfuls of the cookie mixture onto prepared trays without overcrowding and bake for approximately 10 minutes until golden. Cool completely on the trays. The consistency should be soft when they come out of the oven and set as they cool.
6. Store in plastic container with a good fitting lid or a biscuit tin with a lid. They will last for about a week.

These cookies can also be baked in different shapes. Place a cookie shape of choice on to the baking tray and press some of the cookie mixture into the shape. Carefully remove the cookie shape before baking.

Hot Chocolate

(Gluten/WheatFree)

Serves 4

4 level tablespoons pure raw cacao powder

4 tablespoons coconut sugar

1 teaspoon vanilla bean paste

1 L (32 fl oz) milk

pinch cinnamon (optional)

marshmallows (optional)

1. Place all the ingredients into a blender or food processor and blend on high speed for about 30–40 seconds until you have a smooth consistency.
2. Pour into a medium saucepan and gently heat until hot.
3. Serve with or without marshmallows.

You may have to adjust the level of sweetness to suit your taste. Keep in mind that raw cacao is chocolate in its purest form. It is naturally fermented and dried without the use of any sugar or fat. This preserves its many natural nutrients. This is why this is chocolate is actually good for you.

Blueberry and Chia Sorbet Icy Poles

(Gluten/Wheat Free)

Makes 10–12

500 g (16 oz) fresh or frozen
    blueberries
75 g (2½ oz) coconut sugar
500 ml (16 fl oz) coconut
    water
juice 1 lemon
2 tablespoons chia seeds

1. Place blueberries, sugar and water into a saucepan and bring to the boil. Reduce the heat to low and simmer covered for about 5–7 minutes until the sugar has dissolved. Cool completely.
2. Place the blueberries and their syrup into a blender or food processor with the lemon juice and puree until smooth. If you like your sorbet to have some texture, pulse blend for a short time only.
3. Stir in the chia seeds and leave to stand for about 10 minutes stirring the mixture with a fork 2–3 times during that time.
4. Pour into individual icy pole molds with wooden sticks and freeze until set or, if you would like a sorbet, transfer the mixture to an ice-cream maker and prepare as per the manufacturer's instructions.

Depending on how tart the blueberries are, you may need to adjust the amount of sweetener used. Blueberries contain a very high amount of antioxidants. They can be substituted with cherries or mixed berries if you prefer.

Yogurt, Strawberry, Chia and Almond Icy Poles

Makes 10–12

60 g (2 oz) natural almond kernels, skin on
450 g (16 oz) unsweetened, thick Greek-style yogurt
1 tablespoon chia seeds
2 tablespoons maple syrup or agave syrup
1 teaspoon vanilla bean paste
250 g (9 oz) fresh strawberries
6 x 125 ml (4 fl oz) paper or plastic cups
6 wooden lollipop sticks

1. Add the almonds to a food processor and blend until very finely chopped.
2. Place the yogurt into a bowl with the almonds, chia seeds, maple syrup and vanilla. Gently mix together. Taste and adjust the level of sweetness to suit.
3. Wash and hull the strawberries then cut into small pieces and fold through the yogurt.
4. Fill the paper cups to the top with the yogurt mixture and place a wooden stick in the middle.
5. Place in the freezer and freeze until firm.
6. To remove from the molds, dip in hot water for few seconds then run sharp knife along the edge. Icy poles should come out easily.

You can use whatever fruit you like, even a mixture of different fruits.

SUPERFOOD FOR BABIES

Macaroni and Broccoli Cheese
Quinoa, Semolina and Apple Porridge
Chicken with Lentils and Vegetables
Quinoa Bolognaise
Sweet Potato, Broccoli and Avocado Mash
Fish, Broccoli and Corn Mash
Minced Beef, Quinoa and Veggie Puree
Baby Finger Sticks

Macaroni and Broccoli Cheese

Makes 6–8 servings

125 g (4 oz) macaroni (or other very small pasta)

500 ml (16 fl oz) water, approximately

125 g (4 oz) broccoli florets

1–2 teaspoons butter

1 tablespoon Parmesan or other cheese, grated

1. Add water to a medium sized saucepan and bring to a rapid boil. Add the pasta and cook for about 3–5 minutes depending on the size of the pasta you are using.
2. Add the broccoli and continue cooking until the pasta is really soft and the broccoli is cooked and starts to break up.
3. Stir the pasta every now and then as it is cooking to help break up the broccoli and mix through the pasta.
4. Drain using a fine sieve and reserve some of the cooking liquid.
5. Return the pasta and broccoli to the pot, stir in the butter and cheese and as much of the cooking liquid as needed to have a soft (not dry) consistency.
6. Divide leftovers into portions and store in freezer.

This macaroni cheese was loved by my children when they were babies and now it is a favorite with their babies. They started having this at around 7–8 months and they have all loved the Parmesan cheese though any other cheese can be used.

Quinoa, Semolina and Apple Porridge

Makes about 4 tablespoons

1 pink lady apple
250 ml (8 fl oz) water
pinch cinnamon (optional)
2 tablespoons quinoa flakes
1 tablespoon fine semolina
125 ml (4 fl oz) milk
½–2 teaspoons raw sugar
  (optional)

1. Peel and coarsely grate the apple and place into a small saucepan with the cinnamon, (if used), and the water.
2. Bring to the boil, reduce the heat and cook on low heat for 5–8 minutes until the apple is cooked and soft.
3. Stir in the quinoa and semolina and cook for another 5–7 minutes stirring fairly regularly until the flakes and semolina have dissolved and there are no lumps. The apple will soften as you stir and will turn into a puree.
4. Stir in most of the milk and continue to cook for 1 minute. The mixture should be a soft consistency. Add the remaining milk if necessary. You can add more milk if you prefer a more runny consistency.
5. Any leftover porridge will keep in the fridge for 1–2 days, just add a little milk and re-heat.

Depending on the tartness of the apple, you may feel that you need to add some sweetness. If that is the case you may like to start with ½ teaspoon of sugar and build up from there if you feel necessary.

Chicken with Lentils and Vegetables

(Gluten/Wheat Free)

Makes 1 small bowl

90 g (3 oz) white quinoa, rinsed and drained

250 ml (8 fl oz) water

2 tablespoons red lentils

125 g (4 oz) chicken

1 medium potato, peeled and chopped

1 small carrot, peeled and chopped

1 medium courgette (zucchini), top and tailed, chopped

6–8 fresh beans, string removed

375 ml (12 fl oz) water

1. Add quinoa to a small saucepan with the water. Bring to the boil then reduce the heat. Cover and simmer on low heat for 10 minutes until all the water is absorbed and the quinoa is cooked and soft. Add a little more water if the water dries out before the quinoa is cooked. Remove from the heat and leave to stand, covered for about 10 minutes.
2. Place lentils in a fine sieve and rinse under a cold running tap until the water runs clear. Drain well.
3. Place the chicken, potato, carrot, courgette, beans, lentils and water into a small saucepan. Bring to the boil and skim off any froth.
4. Reduce the heat and simmer covered on low heat for about 15 minutes until the chicken is cooked and the vegetables are tender.
5. Once cooked, remove as much of the broth from the pot as possible and set aside.
6. Puree the chicken and vegetables with 3 tablespoons of the cooked quinoa and as much of the cooking broth that is needed to get the consistency you require.

The remaining cooked quinoa can be frozen in small amounts to use as needed. Depending on age of your baby, you may wish to stir in the quinoa rather than pureeing with the chicken and vegetables. This introduces a bit of texture to baby's food. Freeze in portion sizes to use as required.

Quinoa Bolognaise

(Gluten/Wheat Free)

Makes about 1½ small bowls

1–1½ tablespoons extra virgin olive oil

½ medium onion, coarsely grated

1 small clove of garlic, finely grated

200 g (7 oz) finely minced beef

1 small carrot, finely grated

2 tablespoons tomato paste

1 stalk kale or small handful baby spinach

500 ml (16 fl oz) hot water

90 g (3 oz) quinoa, rinsed and drained

Parmesan or other cheese, finely grated (optional)

1. Heat the oil in a medium sized saucepan. Sauté the onion and garlic until just golden.
2. Stir in the mince and carrot and cook until the mince is sealed all over and the carrot is tender. Add the tomato paste and cook for 1–2 minutes.
3. In the meantime, remove and discard the stalk from the kale and thoroughly wash the leaves then chop. (For baby spinach, wash only.)
4. Add the kale to the mince with the water and puree in a blender until you have a fine consistency. Return to the heat, bring back to the boil and add the quinoa.
5. Reduce the heat, cover and simmer for about 20 minutes until the quinoa is cooked. Remove from the heat and leave to stand covered for at least 10 minutes.
6. Serve with cheese if desired. Store leftovers in the freezer in small amounts to be used when needed.

You can substitute the beef with chicken or veal mince. I usually mix in a little cheese before serving and it is usually Parmesan but that is a personal choice and what your baby likes. I prefer to use the white quinoa for this as it cooks quicker and is softer so very suitable for babies.

Sweet Potato, Broccoli and Avocado Mash

(Gluten/Wheat Free)

Makes 1 small bowl

350 g (12 oz) sweet potato (kumera)
200 g (7 oz) broccoli
1 avocado
1 teaspoon butter (optional)

1. Preheat the oven to 200°C (400°F). Place the unpeeled sweet potato on a small baking tray that has been lined with non-stick baking paper and bake for about 30–40 minutes until cooked and soft.
2. In the meantime, cook the broccoli until quite tender and soft enough to be mashed with a fork.
3. When the sweet potato is cooked, peel and mash with a fork with the cooked broccoli and avocado. Stir in the butter while the mixture is still warm (if using)—it adds a little more flavor and richness.
4. Use what you need. Divide the rest into portion sizes and freeze until needed.

The sweet potato can be boiled, steamed or microwaved. I prefer to bake it as it gives the potato more flavor and all of my grandbabies love baked sweet potato. You can add some cooked quinoa or rice to the above recipe. To cook quinoa rinse one part quinoa under cold running water, drain and place into a saucepan with 2 parts water. Bring to the boil, reduce the heat, cover and simmer for about 10 minutes until all the water has been absorbed. Leave to stand for about 10 minutes to fluff up. It's a good idea to cook about more than you need and freeze the leftover for use later.

Fish, Broccoli and Corn Mash

(Gluten/Wheat Free)

Makes about 1 small bowl

150 g (5 oz) broccoli florets

1 medium potato, peeled and diced

1 medium carrot, peeled and diced

1 small clove garlic, finely grated

75 g (2½ oz) fresh or frozen corn kernels

375 ml (12 fl oz) water

125 g (4 oz) fresh white boneless fish fillets

1. Place all ingredients (except the fish) into a medium saucepan. Bring to the boil, cover and simmer on gentle heat for about 15 minutes until the vegetables are quite tender.
2. Add the fish and simmer for another 5–7 minutes until the fish is cooked and flakes quite easily. Drain and reserve the cooking liquid.
3. Puree the fish and vegetables with enough of the cooking liquid until you have a soft puree. Depending on the age of the baby, you can mash the fish and vegetables with a fork instead of pureeing.
4. Keep in the refrigerator for up to 2 days or freeze in portion sizes until needed.

Make sure the fish is super fresh. For added goodness stir in 1–2 tablespoons of cooked quinoa. You can also vary the vegetables—including a green vegetable I feel is always a must.

Minced Beef, Quinoa and Veggie Puree

(Gluten/Wheat Free)

Makes about 1 bowl

2 small stalks Cavolo Nero (Tuscan) kale

2 tablespoons quinoa, rinsed and drained

150 g (5 oz) lean minced beef

1 large potato, peeled and chopped

200 g (7 oz) butternut pumpkin (squash), peeled and cubed

180 g (6 oz) sweet potato (kumara), peeled and cubed

1 small handful baby spinach leaves

375 g (12 fl oz) water

1. Thoroughly wash the kale. Remove the entire stalk then finely chop the leaves and place into a medium sized saucepan.
2. Add the quinoa, mince, potato, pumpkin, sweet potato, spinach and water.
3. Bring to the boil, reduce the heat and simmer on low heat for about 20–25 minutes until the mince and vegetables are cooked. Drain into a fine sieve and reserve the liquid.
4. Puree the mince, quinoa and vegetables with as much of the cooking broth that is needed to get the consistency that best suits your baby.
5. If your baby is a little older, can manage chewing and likes some texture in his/her food, chop the kale and spinach very finely before cooking and after cooking finely mash everything together with a fork.
6. Keep in the refrigerator for about 3–4 days or freeze in portion sizes until needed.

Whenever cooking kale in baby food, I prefer to use the Cavolo Nero (Tuscan) variety as the leaves are a lot more tender and break up more during cooking more than the curly variety.

Baby Finger Sticks

Makes about 15

125 g (4 oz) all-purpose (plain) flour

½ teaspoon baking powder

45 g (1½ oz) quinoa flakes

2 tablespoons coconut sugar

pinch cinnamon (optional)

1 extra large egg yolk

2 tablespoons coconut oil, melted

1 teaspoon vanilla extract

60 ml (2 fl oz) whole milk (or formula)

1. Preheat the oven to 160°C (325°F). Grease and line a baking tray with non-stick baking paper.
2. Sift together the flour and baking powder in a bowl. Mix in the quinoa flakes, coconut sugar and cinnamon (if used). Break up any lumps in the sugar.
3. Lightly whisk together the egg yolk, coconut oil, vanilla and milk. Add to the dry ingredients and mix to form a dough. Add a little extra flour if dough is too sticky.
4. Roll out dough to about 1 cm (½ inch) thickness and cut into sticks.
5. Place on prepared tray and bake for about 15 minutes. If you want a harder biscuit, allow to cook for a further 5 minutes but keep an eye on them as they can brown quickly.
6. Cool completely and store in an airtight container.

My grandchildren loved these when they were teething.

Index

Acknowledgements

A very special thank you to my beautiful publisher and dear friend, Linda Williams, who has always been and continues to be there for me. Thank you also to Fiona Schultz, Managing Director of New Holland who along with Linda has continued to support and encourage all my work. Without both of you and the trust you have shown in me, none of my books would have been possible.

A very special thank you to Victor Yoog from New Holland for his tireless work promoting my books. Nothing ever seems to be too much trouble for you, Victor and all your efforts are very much appreciated.

To the rest of the special team at New Holland, Olga Dementiev, Susie Stevens, Lorena Susak, Jessica McNamara, Diane Ward, Lucia Donnelly, Lesley Pagett, Coral Khun and all of the staff, thank you so much. You are all always so helpful and a joy to work with.

To my very talented photographer Sue Stubbs, thank you so much for the gorgeous photos. This is our fourth book together and you always manage to showcase my recipes to perfection. Thank you also to Imogene Roache for styling the recipes. It was such a pleasure to work with both of you.

Lastly to my wonderful and loving family: husband Graeme, my children Alex, Nikki and Christopher, their other halves, Lachlan, Marcus and Carolyn, and to my all-important tasting panel, the grandchildren Madison, Kobe, Isaac, Hudson and Cooper. Thank you too to my parents. It's wonderful to always have such a supportive family there for me. I am truly blessed.

First published in 2016 by New Holland Publishers Pty Ltd
London • Sydney • Auckland

The Chandlery Unit 704 50 Westminster Bridge Road London SE1 7QY United Kingdom
1/66 Gibbes Street Chatswood NSW 2067 Australia
5/39 Woodside Ave Northcote, Auckland 0627 New Zealand

www.newhollandpublishers.com

A record of this book is held at the British Library and the National Library of Australia.

ISBN 9781742578200

Managing Director: Fiona Schultz
Publisher: Linda Williams
Project Editor: Susie Stevens
Designer: Lorena Susak
Photography: Sue Stubbs
Food Stylist: Imogene Roache
Proofreader: Jessica McNamara
Production Director: Olga Dementiev

Printer: Toppan Leefung Printing Limited

10 9 8 7 6 5 4 3 2 1

Keep up with New Holland Publishers on Facebook
www.facebook.com/NewHollandPublishers